A WEALTH O

D0120766

Susan Hemmings is a journalist, editor and women's rights worker. She became a member of *Spare Rib* magazine collective (1977-1983), where she worked to increase contributions from and for girls and young women, and then older women. She is also a founder member of the Older Feminist Network, 1981. She is editor of the prize-winning *Girls are Powerful* (Sheba, 1982) which won the Other Book Award. Mother of a nineteen-year-old daughter, Susan Hemmings lives in London.

SUSAN HEMMINGS

A WEALTH OF EXPERIENCE

The Lives of Older Women

PANDORA PRESS

London, Boston, Melbourne and Henley

The work of putting this book together is dedicated to Norma Pitfield, Margaret Haine, and to my mother, Mary Pike

First published in 1985
by Pandora Press (Routledge & Kegan Paul plc)

14 Leicester Square, London WC2H 7PH, England

9 Park Street, Boston, Mass. 02108, USA

464 St Kilda Road, Melbourne,
Victoria 3004, Australia and

Broadway House, Newtown Road,
Henley-on-Thames, Oxon RG9 1EN, England

Set in Imprint, 9 on 11pt
by Saildean Ltd., Surrey
and printed in Great Britain
by Cox and Wyman Ltd., Reading, Berks.

Introduction, editorial matter and selection © Susan Hemmings 1985
All other matter © Routledge & Kegan Paul 1985

No part of this book may be reproduced in
any form without permission from the publisher,
except for the quotation of brief passages
in criticism

Library of Congress Cataloging in Publication Data

A wealth of experience, the lives of older women.
Includes bibliographies.
1. Middle aged women – Great Britain – Biography.
2. Aged women – Great Britain – Biography. I. Hemmings, Susan
HQ1059.5.G7W4 1985 305.2'44'0922 [B] 84-16637

British Library CIP data also available

ISBN 0-86358-031-9

Contents

Acknowledgments

Many thanks to all the contributors for much hard work talking, transcribing, writing, re-writing and editing. Besides the contributors with chapters in the book, extensive work on specific pieces was carried out by Roisin Boyd, Valerie Carpenter, Debbie Dickinson, Soreh Levy and Kerry Yeung. Extra research, support and administrative help came from Jan Russell, Kate Flannery, Judith Shaw, and Esther Mayer's daughter. Thanks also to *Spare Rib* magazine for permission to reprint Daphne Mimmack's piece, 'Strong Love, Strong Grief,' which originally appeared in *Spare Rib* issue 134.

Introduction

Susan Hemmings

Women of 40 to 65 have received little positive attention. There are occasional books and television programmes about the menopause, or cheerful reminders that it's possible to take up a mid-life career, or that there really is life after divorce. Matters of interest and importance indeed. But we need to look at the whole range of influences that shaped our lives, and how we in turn have influenced the world. How and why, for example, did so many of us end up married, almost against our better judgment? How did the two world wars affect us? How did we participate in the spread of socialist ideas, and what are our reactions to the subsequent sad decline of the left's idealism? Where do we fit into the changing face of women's liberation this century? This book is a patchwork of personal histories and political commitments which can help us to identify some common roots and shared causes, matters of particular relevance to an age-group whose energy is all too often ignored or sabotaged.

I hope, then, that this book will break new ground. The contributors speak of their lives to combine moving personal testimony with ideas about public and social matters. My intention was for the book as a whole to reflect some of the best characteristics of oral history, such as the release of knowledge and experience of people normally silenced and unpublished, in a form that would have a wide and lively appeal. But I wanted it to go further, enabling the contributors to have the opportunity to reflect, and to develop, if they wished, upon the relative transience of the spoken word. This can only be done when contributors themselves have time to think through their pieces in relation to the whole book, and take on an editorial role themselves. This process has resulted in the book having a strong literary content and a conscious political purpose. I wanted to move beyond individual testimony to a conscious revelation of shared experience that could speak directly to the present and future. This approach has, I hope, also enabled us to rise above the level of 'victim' so often ascribed to middle-aged women. Although the book chronicles considerable pain, disappointment and plain frustration, it is vibrant with optimism for change, and is much, much more than a survival handbook!

Although the book focuses on the lives of women between the ages of 40 and 65, it starts off with the perspectives of two women who are considerably older, to give us a context and a setting. The experiences of women over 65 justify a book entirely of their own. Although they by far outnumber men in that age-group, they are still mainly seen as 'widows' and 'pensioners' wives', and the public face of the pensioners' rights movement is far too often male. There is no effort, as yet, from agencies working with and for pensioners, or within the male-dominated pensioner movement, to define this age-group's needs and issues using gender as a perspective, although it is hard to see how they manage to avoid the issue. One argument they use is that, since pensioners nearly all *are* women, there is no problem of discrimination. Somehow, presumably, years of being seen as secondary to men ceases to be a problem when most of the men of your age-group die. A rather drastic solution, one might think, to sexism. In any case, women's lives are not controlled only by men within the same age-group as themselves. Hopefully, much more attention, and money, will be spent on this matter in the next few years.

In my experience, younger women with an awareness of ageism tend to speak of all of us over about 45 as older women.

However, women of 80 have daughters of 60, and granddaughters in their 40s! Lumping us all together into one generation means we all lose out. Our 'middle years' issues become lost, while the achievements of the women who fought earlier this century, before we were even born in many cases, for suffrage, for internationalism, socialism and peace, abortion and birth control, sink further back into the past than need be.

Why has there been such a silence about our age-group of women? In society in general, and not just in Britain, a middle-aged woman is denoted as a bit of a loser. First, of course, she is no longer sexually viable, or so she is continually told. If married, she'll be awkward, 'going through the change', 'unable to face her children leaving home', and unconfident about just about everything. If she's unmarried – oh dear! Not much chance from that point of view, and again, she'll be a rather sad creature, or a bossy business woman. We're never seen as strong, influential members of society who might have an able contribution to make (unless we happen to be the exception to the rule). Meanwhile, why have our issues and concerns made few inroads into the women's movement, where we might expect to see them being taken up?

The women's liberation movement as we know it today got under way in the late 1960s and through the early 1970s – just as most of us were up to our necks in children – babies to teenagers. We were working, mainly to make ends meet, keeping our marriages going, looking after relatives (often his), with hardly time to turn around. Some of us, not born here, arrived as young women with high expectations, and found open hostility or indifference. Most of us had got married young, giving up jobs or training, or had in any case missed the educational boat. Whatever our backgrounds, most of us were busy taking second or third place to the men and children in our lives, and were becoming accustomed to having our ideas and opinions ignored. If we were born Black or working-class we'd have even less chance of being heard outside the family. Certainly we *knew* about women's lot and women's rights. We'd sometimes been educated and influenced by strong women teachers (often unmarried) who'd handed down to us feminist ideals, and encouraged us. Many of our mothers, too, remembered tough fights, for the vote, for equal pay, for contraception. But despite everything, we slid into the same traps which had caught them, and lost confidence in ourselves as separate and autonomous people.

Meanwhile the women's movement began on a crest of energy from (mainly) young, single, white and middle-class university women frustrated by sexist constraints in the professions: journalism, medicine. These were also the women who had every expectation to 'do well', and who were, instead, coming up against white male bastions on every side. Such women often had access to feminist and other radical texts coming from America, where the Black, gay and women's liberation movements were under way, and the time to read and discuss them. Unless we were exceptionally lucky, we had neither the time, the money, the context, nor the confidence to study these, and if there were meetings, oh the problems with babysitting arrangements, or husbands who felt threatened by us going to women's groups!

The 'whiteness' and the middle-class dominance of the movement, for which it is still paying the price, also made it a place where Black and working-class women, however politically active, would not choose to take their energies. That first tremendous burst of energy, productive as it was for the women's movement, unwittingly excluded many of us who, although just as concerned about women's rights, could not or would not for one reason or another, count ourselves in. There were also those of us who remained convinced (at least on some level) that we *were* liberated, and had no need of a movement. When we compared ourselves to our mothers, we were 'better' educated, had 'chosen' a husband, childbirth . . . it was only later that we began to sense that something was very wrong.

However, some of us did just about manage to get involved in the movement – in our late 20s. The result is that the upper age-range of contemporary movement feminists is around 45. Any woman older than this within the movement has been treated there much as she is outside it: as cranky, boring, bossy, neurotic, and politically backward. There's a kind of tension in groups when she speaks in case she wanders off the point, or says something outrageously reactionary. In social venues older feminists often find it hard to feel at home: we *mind* that we can't hear each other speak, and that we can't see each other in the dark. Things are now improving, but only because we are starting to find the confidence to form ourselves together in groups. Time is for once on our side: feminists like everyone else grow older, and this means that more and more of us are pressing for our own needs to be recognised.

For all the problems of exclusivity of the women's movement, the point of this book is not to take pot-shots at feminists and feminism. Far from it. As many contributors say in their pieces, the women's movement, or women's groups, or women friends, have been our sanity and our salvation in a misogynist world. We've all been driven on by a belief in women's strengths and rights. Whether or not contributors to this book call themselves feminists (many do not) all are acutely aware of the particular power of women, and how men and society have tried to thwart us.

What have been the particular characteristics of our generation? How have we been shaped by a society which while proclaiming a 'sexual revolution' of the 1960s almost universally pressurises women to look 'youthful', that correlates sexuality with youth, and scrapheaps the rest of us as non-sexual beings? This is the society too that, when we were young, educated some of us to expect to 'achieve', but still required us to take second place to our brothers and our husbands; that told us we could choose whether to stay at home or go to work, but expected us all to get married. We were expected to juggle everything –

housework, paid work, childcare, husband-care: then just as things start to ease with the children growing up, it's care of parents, the redundant or ailing husband, the bored and upset unemployed teenagers. All this just when we thought we might take a little time for ourselves, or simply get a job. And, for those of us contributing to the trade union movement despite the odds against us, we are the ones who continue to see both women and women's issues excluded, to the point where we may have despaired that 'trade unionist' will ever be pictured as a woman.

For the very oldest of us, there are memories and influences in our lives of the First World War and its dreadful devastations. For the youngest, there were experiences of seeing our parents (often themselves hardly recovered from the impact of an adolescence marred by the First World War) enduring the second one, going without proper food and clothing for our sakes during endless rationing. We are the ones who benefited from the National Health Service being set up during our childhoods; we are the ones separated from each other by the 1944 Education Act, which picked some of us out of the working classes and lower middle classes and earmarked us for a 'better' life, class-separating us from our (proud) parents, while consigning the huge majority to the bottom of the heap, spoiling our chances for good at eleven years, whatever our true ability.

We, too, are the ones who, using unreliable contraception, found ourselves pregnant by mistake, married or unmarried, and often went through terrible times and risked our lives to get an abortion. At the Family Planning Clinic, if unmarried, we would go through charades to 'prove' we were engaged; at the doctor's, pregnant, we'd have to pretend we were mad.

Meanwhile we joined, with enthusiasm, the revolutionary left parties, both before and after the Second World War; flocked into the peace movement of the 1950s, and were abused and arrested on CND demonstrations, told umpteen times to 'go and live in Russia'. We are also the ones who came to an alien England, to escape Nazism, and then to find that the majority of the English, despite the war, knew next to nothing about the suffering of the Jews, or Jewish culture. Others came to England from India, or the Caribbean, mistakenly expecting something positive here and met with open and racist hostility, while struggling to find housing and jobs, keeping families together.

What, then, despite all our differences in background, are our shared experiences? Marriage! It comes up over and over again, plunged into with reasons that had very little to do with 'love', though much to do with an imposed idea of 'romance', and even more to do with economics, and a search for security which enabled us to get away from home. Some of the contributors chronicle a sharing of love, care, responsibilities: most tell of agonising incompatibilities, or a give and take which turned out mainly to be at the woman's expense. Even in reasonably 'good' marriages, women describe how they have for years suppressed their own needs and intellect in order to preserve their husbands' sense of self. Since our generation lived in an era which was still telling us to 'work' at difficult marriages and to 'make the best of it', some pieces tell of the guilt at wanting a divorce: several point out the economic difficulties for women wanting independence when they have no training, and when their earnings have all gone to the joint household. Others point to the problems of retirement pensions – when you discover your rights are inhibited by your failure to pay independent contributions. The importance for women of seeking training and further education (and its importance as a route out of marriage) is several times underlined.

Almost all the pieces mention the theme of being pulled two (or more) ways: between authoritarian husband and demanding teenage children; between political work and meetings and family responsibilities; between one's own need to survive (work, health, emotions) and cries for help from within the family. It is perhaps these pressures, above all, that result in stories that, on the one hand, are patterns of amazing resilience and maturity, and on the other of depression and debilitating illness – barely noticed by the ever emotionally hungry family! I felt at one stage that I had material for another book I'd call *Women and Asthma* because of the frequency with which this illness was popping up in women's lives. Often we've had to nurse members of the family while literally at death's door ourselves; two contributors who are cancer-survivors tell of this exacting experience.

The middle years are often those in which we are first acutely bereaved, even though many of us have been affected by deaths from the wars when young. Where wars are now being waged, as in Ireland, women are losing children, friends, lovers and live in constant fear of losing more. Many talk about those griefs, facing the loss of parents, a child, dear friends, of coming to some kind of terms with the Nazi atrocities which wiped out whole families, while at the same time keeping everything else going at home and at work. In fact, you may get the sense, when reading the pieces, that the overall theme is 'keeping on going' despite everything.

Is it all bleak then? Are we downtrodden victims on an uphill struggle through endless draining obligations, with no returns? Apparently not. Work can bring great satisfaction. Courses are taken, and passed. Children (often conceived in a far from positive frame of mind) are passionately loved and enjoyed – as are grandchildren. They may disappoint us by, as one writer puts it, making the same mistakes as we did. There is, however, a great deal to learn from them. More than one mother speaks admiringly of a daughter's political energy, and of her influence. Overall, there's a sense of achievement in pulling through, and the experience of an unfolding maturity that comes through hard times and complex situations.

There are women who never experienced 'maternal desire', and others who never wanted to get married: these are also in the book. There's a recognition, too, that it's better to be without a lover, husband, family than to find yourself stuck in an alienating relationship in which you can feel very much alone. There's also the excitement at finding you can happily live on your own, or in a radically different set-up, after being in a conventional marriage for a quarter of a century.

There's plenty of proof here that, despite the economic pressures and the fear of being alone, despite the intense taboos against living outside the conventional family, we can and do disentangle ourselves from miserably incompatible relationships. Several women point out that for years everybody else thought their marriages were perfect, and the cracks were not even visible to family and friends. This must be very common. Three women took the courageous stand of changing or reclaiming their sexuality after twenty or more years of marriage, and becoming lesbians. This must serve as a reminder of all the many thousands of married lesbians still living with their husbands. There was no real choice for us in a world where heterosexual relationships in general and marriage in particular were (and still are) presented as women's only possible sexual future. Singleness was stigmatised, and lesbianism even more so to the extent that most of us didn't even know it was a possibility.

Religion, too, is a frequent theme in the book. It was common for many women of our generation to have instilled into us by at least one parent, and at school, one of the brands of the Christian patriarchy. Meanwhile women of other religious and cultural backgrounds had their beliefs either ignored or despised in Britain. Several writers tell of their long struggle to throw out the more insidious parts of their indoctrination, and their efforts, shared with others in the book, to explore the possibilities of a new and unimposed spirituality for themselves.

Links between age and disability are also brought out. Ablebodied people tend to think that disability belongs to the disabled, and won't happen to them. But along the continuum of age more and more of us will experience disabling illness, which may arrive in a sudden and devastating form, or more gradually.

The qualities of courage and modesty are shared by all the contributors. In their book of interviews about older women's lives, *Dutiful Daughters* (1977), Jean McCrindle and Sheila Rowbotham say, 'All the women were diffident at the beginning, finding it hard to believe that their lives could be interesting to anyone but themselves and their families.' I had exactly the same experience: each of the contributors said to me in one way or another, 'Why me? I'm not interesting. I haven't been through anything very difficult, or achieved anything very much. What's more, I can't write very well.' Older women are simply not used to anyone taking an interest, or in believing we have anything worthwhile to say about the world. Then there was the considerable problem for them of how to be frank about their lives: it does not come easily to older women, who have often spent decades supporting and nurturing the flagging egos of those around them, to speak harshly or critically of family life. Women felt they might be disloyal in pointing out the less desirable parts of a marriage to a man they also loved. The reader, too, may have reservations about such passages: the contributors will depend on your sensitive response to the personal revelations they make, not just to dis-burden themselves, but in the cause of uncovering some of the roots which can rot and bring a relationship tumbling down. Wherever we have felt anxious about repercussions on relatives or friends, women have used other names both for themselves and within their accounts. If you tell a true story – and what other kind would have been right for this book? – you have to take risks. We need to break the silence, stop pretending that we feel fine when really we're being slowly stifled, and we must start to uncover the complexities that often lie under a veneer of orderliness or 'normality'.

Although this book belongs to the contributors, I take responsibility for the omissions I know must have occurred. The book's limitations will reflect mine, not theirs. It was not possible to produce something totally comprehensive or representative. I am worried, of course, that there might be some serious lack. But I look forward with no trepidation at all to any critiques which say that the book lacks the voice of 'ordinary women'. That voice permeates the book. And to those who feel that the book is negative about marriage, I reply that I, too, was surprised by my contributors' disenchantment, and by the suffering they'd endured. I looked for more positive evidence of marriage's joys and rewards: I could not find it. Finally, this is not a book about 'achievers' in the business or professional worlds, even though some of the writers have done well in those areas. It's a book about women who care for women and humanity and who see that commitment, in a general sense, as being on the left of the political spectrum, as I do myself. While 'success' and 'happiness' for ourselves as individuals is part of our liberation, most of all this book is about improving conditions for all women, everywhere.

I hope this book helps to put us more on the map. Thanks to all my inspirational older women friends, and to the contributors, and to the Older Feminist Network, who have given me and each other so much support and affection. Here's to us!

CHAPTER 1

A View of the Century – Working for Better Times

Henrietta Hempstead

I was born in 1900, the eldest of a family of six children. When I was nearly 2, my parents moved from Halifax to Leeds to become caretakers of a Methodist church. This provided living accommodation, but we had no money, and Dad had to go out and sell his coat to buy flour and other food so that Mother could bake and make bread. As time went on we lived in other houses, always back-to-backs with one living room, two bedrooms and a cellar. Everything was done in the living room: washing, cooking, baths in front of the fire. The six of us were born within eleven years. Closets [toilets] had to be shared with two other neighbours. We used open middens because there were no dustbins, tipping in all our household rubbish, which was collected in carts. Toilets were flushed once a week by men from the council. Dad was by now working as a labourer in an engineering firm, on wages of about 18 shillings a week. I don't know how we survived – but we had good parents who cleaned, cooked, mended boots and shoes and clothes. A hard life: but we did not know how hard, because most people around us were in the same conditions.

All through my childhood I used to listen in the crowded living room to the discussions of some of my aunts and uncles who came to visit us. Most of them were in some trade, and one of my uncles was an interpreter for an engineering firm. He went to Russia for his firm and always had a good word for the men he'd come into contact with there, telling us how terrible their conditions were. This was before the Revolution. I was always very interested in the people of Russia and their history.

My mother herself was never able to go out anywhere as she had no proper outdoor clothes, only a shawl, and some of my uncle's boots. Whenever she had a baby, her sisters paid a neighbour to care for us so that she could stay in bed for ten days, and I would go to my aunt's every day before I went to school to fetch a jug of milk and egg with some whisky as a tonic for her. I used to go washing people's steps at weekends for a penny, to give to my mother.

I started work at 13, twelve hours a day in a mill for 5*s* a week. I had to catch the 5.15 a.m. tram to get to work at 6 a.m. After a while I went to work in an asbestos mill – we did not know the dangers then, and many people in that area have since died of asbestos-related diseases. I remember the mill was just one mass of dust, with all the fibre flying about. I only stayed for a few months, because by 1914 the war had broken out and I went to work in the armaments industry packing cartridge shells and bullets. After two years when I was 16 I joined my Dad, who was now working on the trams, and became a conductor. You had to be 18 really, but they never checked up! Since we were paid more or less equal pay with the men, the money was quite good for those days.

By now we'd moved to a better house, still a back-to-back, and my brothers were beginning to work. Still my mother had such a hard working life, cooking, baking, sewing, cleaning, washing . . . and I remember she always had her windows nice, and we were not allowed to disturb the curtains, and had to take care with the furniture, helping with all the chores, including making the rag rugs to put on the floors.

Of course, by now I was going around with my girl friends. We used to go on a Saturday afternoon to a dancing class, something I didn't tell Dad and Mother. It cost 6*d* a lesson. We decided one Saturday afternoon to take the train to Harrogate, about half an hour's ride. This was a lovely place and still is, and I still visit it when I go and stay with my family in Leeds. We were walking in the gardens and sat on a seat. Two wounded soldiers, sent back from the front to recover, came and sat with us, and of course we talked – and that is how I met my husband, Jim. He had been wounded on the Somme, and had seen many thousands of men killed and wounded. He was one of very few in his company to survive. His mother sent him a pound for his birthday, and he paid for us to go and have some tea. After this he had to go back to his company, where he continued to fight on the front. He was hurt again, gassed this time, and blinded for a while.

I didn't meet him again for 15 months, but we exchanged letters. When he had his leave, he came and asked my parents' permission for me to go with him to his parents' home in Brightlingsea. I never knew that such a lovely place existed! The houses all painted white, the gardens, the sea and the boats – especially after Leeds with all the smoke and muck. Nowadays Leeds is different, a lovely city, because of the Clean Air Act. I spent two of Jim's leaves with him and his parents and they were very nice to me, as were his brothers and sisters. The only work in Brightlingsea was connected to the sea, and Jim did not want to work at sea as it never agreed with him. So when the war finished he came to Leeds and was able to get on the trams. We married when I was 19 and had at first to live with my parents. He enjoyed my family and they also thought a great deal of him. After 18 months we were able to get our own small back-to-back house for 4*s* and 6*d* a week. By that time my son James was six months old, and then five years later I had my daughter, Dorothy. We had taken my mother's advice and used a birth control method. She told me they had learned too late for them to use it, but she gave this advice to all the family when they married. After ten years we were given a council house, and we were thrilled with the bathroom, toilet and garden.

To go back now a few years: when I was 20, and my son was

still very young, I joined the Labour Party Women's Section in Leeds. I was active in this for several years, taking my young children with me to the afternoon meetings, and helping at election times, giving out leaflets. Also at this time my husband went to his union meetings, but after the General Strike of 1926 he seemed to lose faith in the Labour Party leaders, and his political interest waned from then on though he always believed in Labour. During this period clinics were started for mothers to take their babies to, and municipal laundries were started up. These were a great help, saving all the upheaval of washday, and while I went off to do the wash, my husband always helped with the housework or prepared the dinner. At every opportunity we had we went with the children out of the streets for walks in the country. We used to go for miles, with my daughter in the pushchair. If we ever had a shilling to spare, we would occasionally go to the pictures – but wages were still very low and I never had more than £2 a week to pay for everything, and he had a bit of pocket money, about 5*s* a week.

When we settled into our council house I was 30. I thought about joining the Co-operative Women's Guild as I had been a member of the Co-op since I was married. The dividend [the money the Co-op movement pays back to its members from profits made] was very important to us financially. It went towards clothes and an annual week's holiday in Blackpool or Bridlington. We were very lucky because very few people went away on holidays then. My mother had also joined the Guild when we were growing up. I'd come to know some of the women in the Guild through being in the Labour Party. I enjoyed the meetings and through these I learnt about the procedures of how a meeting should be run, and of the aims of the Guild and the Co-operative movement in general. These appealed to me very much and before long I started to take an active part, both locally, and when the Guilds came together in regions, and nationally for rallies. We had some really wonderful speakers, many of them well-educated women who were trying to make women rouse themselves and take part in fighting for a better life for themselves and their families. Peace was always an important theme. I remember once, too, we had Marie Stopes to speak on birth control methods. This was a very controversial subject to take on at that time, but it gave many women the knowledge of how to control their families. This was very important for women at a time when most men didn't approve of, or wouldn't use, contraceptives, as it allowed women to use the cap without their husbands knowing. The council allowed a birth control clinic to be opened in Leeds in about 1935. It was a very progressive Labour council. From the Guild I went on to join the Co-operative Party and here we had a great fight to get members elected to the Co-operative Board of Directors as most of the Directors in Leeds were Conservatives. They were greatly helped to stay in power by the *Yorkshire Post*, plus the fact that they were elected by postal ballot, and it was very difficult to shift them.

All through my 30s I remained busy with the Guild and working for the Co-operative Party. In 1942 my husband became very ill with a burst ulcer and after a long period of work it was made clear to us by the doctor that he could not work again on the trams. But he couldn't leave the job without first being released: the trade union went with him to the tribunal and supported him. After a lot of talking, my son persuaded him to consider returning to Brightlingsea. In the end he agreed, and went there to live with an aunt while he looked for furnished accommodation. I then went to join him, and I'll always remember the kindness of the neighbours. It was 1943, and Brightlingsea had several bombs dropped near where we lived. Many nights my dog and me spent some time under the Morrison shelter – my husband stayed in bed!

I soon joined the Guild again locally, and it being summer I was invited by some of the women I'd got to know at the meetings in their houses to go working on the land, picking peas, cherries and apples. The pay was a shilling an hour, but I enjoyed being in the fields.

My husband was able to find work in the office of a shipyard in Wivenhoe, nearby. When we'd first been married he'd gone to classes at Pitman's College in Leeds and obtained a first class certificate in business training and this helped him to get this clerical job. After about 25 years he was now ever so happy and contented, with regular hours and meals. This was a great improvement for his health, and for me too. Work in transport means one never gets regular mealtimes, and some days I never stopped making meals as the children had to have theirs at the right times.

After the war ended, with help from the Guild and the Co-operative Party I was persuaded to stand for the local council as Labour and Co-operative candidate. I was elected – I don't think they had ever had a woman on the council before. I was able to press them to build council houses, as the Labour Government was giving a lot of help in this respect. We got twenty-four new ones built. I was also elected as their representative on the County Education Committee. During that time, too, we started off the home helps scheme, and I got many local improvements such as a proper bus shelter which is still there today. I did not get re-elected though, and I think this was because I wanted them to move too quickly!

However, I continued with my work in the Guild, and in various political activities. I was elected as manager and governor to Brightlingsea's three schools; I served on the Area Youth Committee, and I was also elected to serve on the Tuberculosis Care Association. I served on these committees for the next 25 years. There was a great deal to be done in improving the schools, and I was determined to see through the building of a new infant and junior school. I'd always wanted a better school life and education for our own children.

All this time though I had to pay all my own expenses, and

while I could I used the money I earned in the work in the fields. But I've been repaid with the satisfaction of seeing the cure for tuberculosis, and hundreds of children in their new school. I've also seen over the years all the good that home helps have brought to the elderly, and how the old have appreciated their kindness.

Remaining active in the Guild I took on district work, and that meant going to Guilds to speak. We were given different papers to study on many subjects affecting women, such as mental health, social security, housing, and on the Co-operative movement nationally and internationally.

Around 1950 my son and his wife and young son came to live in Brightlingsea. They stayed in this area until a few years ago. Doris, his wife, became interested in forming a group of young Co-operators locally called Playways and Pathfinders which became very successful. I became its leader for a few years – very hard work, but I enjoyed it. The Co-operative Education Committee helped a lot, with all kinds of equipment for games. Exhausting – especially the teenagers! I used to come home very tired!

Then I became a member of the Co-operative Education Committee and this meant many conferences and meetings. I became elected as a Director on the Colchester and East Essex Co-operative Board, which of course meant dealing with the trading and business side of the movement. It involved several trips to Europe to exchange ideas, such as the development of supermarkets. Many new shops were built around this time and it was all very interesting to me.

In 1956 I was invited by a group of Women for Peace in Poland to take part in a three weeks' visit to their country with other Women for Peace from walks of life in Britain. I went as a Co-operator. I will never forget the people I met there, and especially the women who had themselves been in concentration camps. Nor will I forget the terrible destruction of the towns, especially Warsaw. What they'd had to face was terrible, and my visit to the Auschwitz concentration camp has always been with me, along with memories of the courage of these women who had survived. We had some pleasurable things to enjoy, too, such as a visit to the opera, and to the home of Chopin, hearing his music played. We met many people in many towns, going into some of their homes, and the children were especially lovely. I took with me a letter from the Directors of our society, and for many years we exchanged letters with one or two of the women. I celebrated my fifty-sixth birthday there, and on a visit to a mill in one town, I was presented with a beautiful handmade lace table cover, while they sang happy birthday. I have the cloth on my table every day since and it is still as lovely as ever.

On my return I went to many Guild meetings, and to the local secondary school, to give a report of my visit. All through this period of trips abroad I'm pleased to say that my husband helped me a great deal. He did his own cooking, washing and cleaning while I was away. All those years previously when I'd first started in the Guild and the children were young I'd had to struggle with myself at leaving him and the children, even to go to a meeting or day conference. I never left the children alone when their Dad was working. But when he was home, and I'd get ready to set off to the Guild, sometimes my daughter would cry, and I'd feel pulled two ways – usually I'd stay home then. But as they became teenagers they themselves joined the Co-operative Youth Club and often joined in with the Women's Guild in social and dancing evenings. So eventually they accepted the Guild and seeing me occasionally go off to conferences. By the time I came down to Brightlingsea of course my son was married and my daughter was working in the Pay Corps, so they were pleased to see I had my own interests. My husband seemed to like my involvement too, though he himself was busy in his leisure time (and later in retirement) with the garden, crosswords, or jigsaws. We often at the weekend had a walk in the country around us, calling in to have a drink occasionally if we could afford it.

Of course, living by the sea many of my family, children, grandchildren, great-grandchildren, have come down for summer trips, and we have had many pleasurable holidays. I've cooked a good many meals over all those summers! I have watched my own family growing, and getting politically involved – and also watched the changes which have brought many young people into politics, especially the Campaign for Nuclear Disarmament, Friends of the Earth, and the fight against unemployment. It gives me great pleasure to see all the number of young people taking part in these movements, and on peace demonstrations. I also greatly admire the women of Greenham Common; I understand why they're there and what they're fighting for. Two of my great-granddaughters have been.

I have been a widow since 1979 when my husband died after 62 years together. It was a sad and difficult last two years together, but at the end, in the final few weeks, I had a lot of support from my daughter and son, and the nurses who came to make him comfortable. After this I had a bad time with shingles, but I was determined to keep going and take an interest in things, and I've particularly kept up my contact with the local school. It is seeing the children which makes me feel how important it is to support CND. When I visit there, I wear my CND badge so that they'll know I'm a supporter. I see plenty of Dads too coming along to see the children's work and talk with the teachers – many more of them today are taking a share in caring for the family, which is very good.

As far as my own health goes, I've been having treatment for pernicious anaemia since 1939. Of course, when I first had it diagnosed there was no National Health Service free treatment, and I had to find the money to pay for every bottle of medicine I had to have. For a time I delivered papers to raise the money, but I couldn't carry on with this. Eventually things did become easier and by the time I came to Brightlingsea I was having treatment three times a week free. Over the years I've seen many kinds of treatment come and go. Now I have an injection of Vitamin B12 every three weeks. All of this had made me thankful to be able to be well and enjoy life, and want to do something in return for all the treatment I've received: that's what is behind a lot of the voluntary work I have done.

On my eightieth birthday my son and his wife paid part of my fare to go with them to the USSR. I have always been interested in the achievements of this country. We travelled 7,000 miles. We went from Moscow to a resort in Georgia on the Black Sea and back to Leningrad. It really was marvellous to see the people, the children in the resorts, and the places they have restored. Owing to the language, we could not talk to the people directly, only through an interpreter, but we made some good friends. Then when I was 82 I made a visit with my daughter to see her son and his wife and child in Vermont in the USA.

When I look around and see the changes that have been made, I know that every one of them has had to be fought for, and I'm pleased to think I've done a small share to bring these about, particularly for women and children. We must all guard against these being taken away again from us. This means involvement in pensioners' matters, too, and since I've been a pensioner, I've worked hard for pensioners' rights. We have good times together in our clubs and the outings and chats are a great pleasure.

I have had a fairly good life – plenty of ups and downs, sadness and happiness. I enjoy reading – through my life I've read most of the classics, always borrowing them from the library, and still do enjoy reading, and I don't like rubbish. We've always taken working-class newspapers – first we had the *Daily Herald* and on Sunday the Co-operative paper, *Reynolds News*; then when these stopped we took the *Daily Worker*, now the *Morning Star*. We always wanted to know what was really happening in the world, not all this nonsense, like with 'Charles and Di'. Television and the radio have enabled me to enjoy good music, symphony concerts, ballet and plays, and to keep up with the news. I like watching sport, but dislike boxing. I've got a good relationship with my neighbours, because now I live on my own this is really necessary. I enjoy my home and try to keep the garden tidy. I do all my own work in the house, cooking, washing and cleaning, and hope I will continue to do so and not be any trouble to the family, or anyone else.

The Co-op has been a very important influence on my life. It's through the Co-operative movement that I've had a political education, with reading, meetings and travel. I believe that co-operatives can provide the answer to many of the problems in the world, especially the Third World. They've been successful in many of the socialist countries. They could also work well here: people are doing something for themselves where profit isn't the *only* motive, which it has to be in the capitalist system. In Co-ops, the profit goes back into improving things for the group. In the Co-operative movement, some of it has been used for education, and in our locality it pays, for example, for the pensioners' groups.

I always think how fortunate I am to live near the sea. I can watch the sailing boats and the cargo ships going up the river to Colchester. Every Sunday after lunch I take the bus for a short ride and walk round the promenade. I look at the whole scene of reflections on the water at sunset, and watch the children doing all the things that children have always done, crabbing and playing in the water and sand.

As I watch them I know that there is still so much to be done – and the most important is to get rid of nuclear missiles and work for peace. I think back over my own life, and know that whatever has been achieved for us all has been fought for, and this is true throughout history. Men and women have made great sacrifices, and are still doing so everywhere in the world, so that people may have a decent life, and live with dignity. If I have been part of that, I am satisfied.

CHAPTER 2

Staying Power

Marion Evans

'Do you believe in fairies?' comes the cry from the stage, and the vast audience of children watching *Peter Pan* choruses 'Yes!'

Few women would consider that the ideas they'd been steeped in since early childhood had any influence on their subsequent plunge into matrimony. Nor would men, for that matter. 'And they all lived happily ever after.' Well, my parents didn't. I've never thought fully about why not. But my recollection is of a never-ending torment, and being twisted into it, even feeling guilty that it could be my fault. I wanted out. Home was cold: a constant discord thwarted and bent development. Only by continually minimising my own sense of self could I lessen the stress that pressed in all around. So, as a way out, I married.

I'd been introduced to a household that seemed all harmony – that would be how my home would be. It was the early 1930s. Like most youngsters then, I did not consider whether we were or were not compatible, whether mature or not, whether we shared aspirations, or whether these might develop. Do youngsters now approach marriage less blindly? I think and I hope there is a somewhat greater chance.

However, I definitely meant to make a success of it. Folk tales of good overcoming evil are part of human heritage, but was it men who put the 'happy ever after' marriage bit in? Maybe in past centuries, when women were men's chattels, this may have seemed true to men, but it has been increasingly an act of self-deception in this century to enter marriage with this presumed ending in mind.

Three children later, delighting in their development in spite of all the fatigue: workhorse days, with the morning spent handwashing in the sink, constant pram-pushing, conjuring sheer magic to feed a family on rations. The war stole much of our own youth – afterwards, life resumed a somewhat easier pattern. We acquired a second-hand car, and moved to a slightly larger house. I could depend on my husband to do any job around the house and garden. It was only later that I saw the limits of that dependability. My confidence was shaken when, under stress of additional work in his job, he nearly cracked. The complete trust I had formerly felt in him was vital to me, the greatest of my needs. Its loss shocked me tremendously.

I often think how surprised he would be to know this. As it is, ours has been largely a marriage of silence. I like to talk things out. He can't. He is generous financially, has always been completely faithful, and many would think it a good marriage. But he is silent. He likes corners. The radio is on – so one mustn't interrupt. The television is on, so we cannot talk. Before television, he used to go frequently to the cinema. Eventually I found the long programmes tedious, so he went alone. He preferred his own company, and I remember saying once, 'So and so is coming round for coffee,' and he replied, 'Why?'

I took a job which involved a lot of standing, and I began to experience extensive back pain. After much to-ing and fro-ing from doctors to hospitals, I was told by two middle-aged doctors that it was probably menopausal and that there was nothing to worry about. Eventually a tumour in the spine was found and treated with radiotherapy. I made a good recovery and the specialist was satisfied I should have no more trouble. I went back to working in a school, a job I quite enjoyed, but once more experienced a spot of trouble, this time with my periods. This eventually led to a visit to a teaching hospital and I was told cauterisation was necessary. I undressed, and while I was lying on the bed, a screen was lowered in front of my face. Soon I heard male voices – a doctor entering with what I presumed to be a group of students to whom he spoke technically. I then experienced a searing pain. 'A woman of 46,' I heard him say. They left. Not a word to me. I felt horrified – I was bleeding. The nurse said, 'You'll be all right in a few hours,' and, when I pressed, gave me sanitary protection. I went home on the bus 'A woman of 46 . . .' echoing in my mind. A shattering experience in every sense, but I don't think I ever mentioned it at home. The whole ignominious experience was unspeakable.

I returned to work. My own children were doing well. My periods became increasingly heavy, and I took to carrying a constant supply of glucose tablets to keep me going. After several particularly bad haemorrhages I remembered how, after the birth of my last child, the consultant told me of a large fibroid in my womb, which would be a nuisance later. It was. It was decided I should have a hysterectomy. Because of the complications, I had a long convalescence – and depression set in. This increased, and I had to give up my job. On returning for a check-up, I remember the surgeon's words, 'The operation will make no difference to your husband.' I often wonder how much difference this pronouncement, this complete exclusion of my feelings, made to the future of my marriage. Perhaps I am abnormally sensitive, but his comment wasn't helpful. What a male view of intimate living! It all seemed to culminate in a depression of considerable magnitude.

Of course, contributing to it all was the disappointment I felt in my marriage from which I had erroneously expected too much. I'd failed to take into account my own inadequacies – both of us expecting that fairy-tale ending, yet with his being brought up in total sexual ignorance these were unreasonable expectations. I, almost as ignorant as he, could not help him. It was all a dismal disappointment.

But because our children flourished, our relationship was and is largely built on our shared affection for them. So in mid-depression, I had to take stock – in that state you have to pull yourself up by your own boot strings. You must get to grips with understanding the underlying cause. Every time since when I have been ill, or deeply disappointed, there has come a time when I've got up, counted the cost, seen what's left and had another go. You either go over – or you go under. Sometimes I am frightened at the interactions between mind and body and wonder if illness is an effort to escape what seem like insurmountable circumstances. If this is so, you must face the situation squarely, and decide on a recovery action. Eventually, I decided to take a new course for myself, and went to art college as a mature student . . . feeling very immature!

This proved a source of real happiness – I felt I should have been doing this work all my life. Soon I was excited to find I had a painting accepted for a major exhibition, and several more successes followed, including a commission. I gained confidence, and began to work on my own at home. Life brightened. We ventured some holidays in Europe, delighting together in new places. Although my husband still felt unable to talk with 'strangers' he began to enjoy the contacts we made then, and through my work, and he has continued to do so.

By now my grown-up family married. One daughter and her husband bought a cottage in the Cotswolds which had a largish annexe, and this we took over for our own use. My husband reached retirement, and became gradually more involved with life at the cottage, working on the smallholding which surrounded it, and becoming part of the village life. This smaller community was more to his liking than the city and a pattern evolved of my spending summers in the country with him, and winters in the city in our flat. These times apart proved very successful, and gave more pleasure in the times we spent together.

I had by now enough work prepared for a one-woman show selling several works and getting a new commission. This freedom to work undisturbed for long periods was very restoring. I had a particularly close friendship in town with the mother of my younger daughter's husband. Eventually, the part of the family we shared the cottage with decided to take up a wonderful job opportunity in Canada. The era of peaceful routine was about to disrupt – they left, we had to sell the cottage and land to help them out, plus the flat in the city, and eventually decided to buy a more modern place in the country. I was to keep on my city life by having a room with the in-law woman friend with whom I was so very close. The new house was idyllic, the laissez faire arrangement to visit my friend just suited. But something as usual was waiting round the bend: this time it was cancer.

Strangely enough I neither felt distressed at the idea of an exploratory operation, nor troubled when I was told the result. I just knew I would get over it. So the healing process began, with fifteen sessions of radiotherapy, and it was with considerable annoyance that after several months, when I should have been well, I still had disturbing symptoms. Shortly after, leaving me profoundly sad, my dear city friend died. My way of easing deep emotional moments is to write, and although the poem I wrote to exorcise my grief gave temporary relief, I still cannot read it without tears.

Soon I was back in hospital with a second operation. Several more weeks in hospital completed the radiotherapy course.

A new start! I was well again. A college friend who was in a London hospital at the same time wrote to me, 'We will recuperate in the spring together.' She did not return home – so within a year I had two very deep griefs.

But I thought of the future, not of past times, and threw myself with vigour into the gardening. The garden had grown very wild during my long stay in hospital when my husband had to spend much of his time and energy travelling to visit me. I naughtily took a pride in neighbours' astonishment that I was able to tackle this work. They seemed to think, by virtue of my illness and my age, that I should 'call it a day'. It was now 1982, and I enjoyed the best of the summer, and my consultant was so pleased with my progress he allowed us to take a much looked-forward-to visit to the family abroad. This was a great joy.

Returning home, and looking forward to Christmas . . . alas, the turkey stayed in the freezer, for on Christmas day my husband was in bed with pneumonia! For two weeks I nursed him night and day, but then a thrombosis threatened his well-being. He spent some time in hospital. His recovery was very slow, learning to walk again with physiotherapy. That was nearly a year ago, since then I have grown in capacity with the job of caring for him, the house, and the garden. What's more, I've learnt to drive the car, passing the stage of feeling sick when I actually get into it!

But I must still take on far more than I expected, and I shall not be at ease until he has regained his former health. Now he enjoys a diversion of company, and even if this means a lot of cooking, which I enjoy anyway, it is worthwhile. I must help him now to fight the depression that comes with progressive arthritis and his illness depriving him of all his former skills. I work on in the faith that, if we remember it, there is a strength far beyond our own as individuals, to help us conquer the defeat so many situations could bring if we denied its presence. Call it what you will – I like very much Galsworthy's poem:

If on a Spring night I went by
And God were standing there
What is the prayer that I would cry
To Him? This is the prayer:
O Lord of Courage grave,
O Master of this night of Spring,
Make in me a heart too brave
To ask Thee anything!

There's still so much I want to do, so much to create. In this piece, of course, I've left so much out, and dealt scantily with other parts. But I've tried to take a step back and look hard at our two lives, bound together in the married state. The glaring truth that emerges is the unequal, and often tangential development of the partners – yet at the same time the great interdependence and need of the other. The answer is in a growth of tolerance – while preserving at the same time the right to fight for personal development. Many problems are insoluble, but because I've learnt about strength, I've found the greater the difficulty, the greater the satisfaction in overcoming it.

CHAPTER 3

Making a Home Away from Home

Joyce Young

I came to England from Jamaica in 1964. I'd been divorced from my husband for six years then but although the marriage was long over, he continued to make a nuisance of himself, visiting and provoking arguments. In addition my eldest daughter wanted to come to England to take up nursing, and my son was wanting to join the RAF. Since I already had a brother and sister living in this country, it seemed the place to choose to emigrate to. Fortunately my brother was able to arrange a job for me here, and the intention was to come on my own at first and live with him until such a time as I could sort myself out, when the children would join me. Meanwhile, they would be cared for by an aunt in Jamaica.

I gave in my notice to the firm where I'd been employed for six years. My boss, who was English, told me he thought I wouldn't like England, because it was so cold and miserable, and would want to return home. With this in mind, he promised to hold my job open for me for six months, and we agreed I'd write to him to let him know if I was returning or not.

I arrived in England on a Sunday morning in November, at 7.30 in the morning. It was cold, dark, strange – especially for a Jamaican who is accustomed to seeing the sun at 6.30 every morning. Although I was sad at having left home and the children, I still felt a certain amount of excitement at being in a new country. That was the first day!

The next morning I had to report for work in Leicester. I left home at seven o'clock. It was a dismal morning with a light fog, dark and rainy. I felt thoroughly miserable. In that moment I wondered what on earth I had come here for. However, I arrived and reported to the company secretary, who was kind enough to say, 'Have two days off, and start on Wednesday.'

I had a very pleasant office overlooking the garden. It was lovely to see all the brown leaves on the ground, because at home there are no seasons – 365 days of summer. But things went badly in that branch. The manager and I couldn't get on and I was moved to the Head Office where I am still working today.

Those early days here were very depressing. The winter mornings were getting colder and darker every day. And besides the weather, life was so very different. There was no one dropping in in the evenings to say hello. You just sat down and watched the television. Very few people had telephones here at the time. I was used to ringing up friends and popping round. In any case, there wasn't anyone here to ring! Life was a boring round of work, coming home, and TV, feeling alone, and missing the children. Reading between the lines of their letters, I could tell they were unhappy. Things just didn't improve, and at the end of six months I'd had it and was ready to go home. I wrote and told the children I wanted to return and that as soon as I had their reply, I'd write to my employers telling them I was coming back. But they wrote begging me not to return because they'd been dreaming of coming to England. Donna was longing to get into a hospital to do her nursing training; Nigel was dreaming of the RAF. They said it was because I was lonely that I was so depressed. Well, I decided to stay, and immediately made arrangements for them to join me.

Eventually they arrived – the two youngest came first, Nigel and Kerry. Donna had to remain a while to sort out what domestic things she could bring for me. They started school in September 1965, Nigel being 15 and Kerry 10. It must have been strange for them. Suddenly there was no one at home to greet them after school and they were coming home with keys on a string around their necks. I remember it was several weeks before Kerry told me her string was too short – she was virtually strangling herself trying to open the door. She had to go inside and lock herself in, very strange for her indeed. After a little longer at my brother's, we moved to my sister's.

We remained there for two years. I helped look after her children as she was the district midwife and was often out at nights. Donna had meanwhile arrived, and was living at my brother's. Eventually my sister became a health visitor, with more normal office hours, and it was time for me to look for our own place.

This was when I really came up against racial prejudice in a strong way. I'd seen a place advertised, and as soon as I'd telephone and they'd hear my voice, they'd say it was just let, or no longer available. It happened so many times every day that the girls in my office decided they would start ringing up making the appointments for me. They'd say; 'I'll get there at six o'clock, please promise to hold it until I get there.' They'd agree, but when I'd knock and they'd open the door, they'd shut it in my face, or occasionally some would say, 'Sorry, it's already let.'

We spent about a year getting doors slammed every which way. Finally I was getting so depressed my boss called me in and said, 'You know, we can see you're not the same person you were – do you want to talk about it?' So I told him what the problem was and he told me he knew of a cottage adjoining one of the company's pubs. 'It's not much of a place,' he said, 'and we don't want to spend any money on it because we're intending to extend the pub into it.' I went to look, and indeed it wasn't much of a place, two rooms up and down, outside toilet, lean-to kitchen, no bathroom. But a place of my own was a joy to have, and I told him I would take it. 'Just one thing, though,' I told him, 'I can't possibly live without a bathroom.' He explained that would need planning permission. I told him I'd noticed that in several homes in this country they had bathtubs in the kitchen with a lid on and that I'd be happy with that. When I went there next not only had he put in such a bath, but hot water, and plumbed it all in!

Despite the fact we had hardly any furniture, we were happy to move in there, making a fire in the grate, sitting around eating fish and chips from the corner shop. The next day we furnished it – if you have to furnish a whole place, you buy cheap pieces. That old furniture served us well for many years until we were able to replace it. Living there had its funny side – rushing out in the cold to the outside toilet, and the upstairs rooms so cold the ice used to form on the windows. In the end we got a storage heater downstairs, and used to undress down there, and rush up straight into bed.

There was a small community of Jamaicans in Leicester, some of whom I met through my sister. She introduced me to people she knew, and I got to know one man in particular who was more or less the centre of the community here. I began to go to meetings where we discussed matters of interest to Jamaicans over here. At that time there was a regular Jamaican programme on Radio Leicester, and a panel of Jamaicans taking part. I joined in with this a few times, though my radio career was very brief, as I did not like the sound of my voice on the air!

At first, while the Jamaican community was relatively small, I remained involved, going to various social functions. However, when it began to grow, the larger it became, the less I felt I belonged. I remember the first time I felt that isolation. I was at a party of about 200 or 300 West Indians. If you haven't ever lived in Jamaica, you won't understand that you can live there for a whole lifetime and never find yourself in a community where everyone except you is Black, because Jamaica is such a multi-racial place. So although I was Jamaican, I felt strange. Perhaps, too, because I was getting older, and wasn't into reggae music (I don't like pop music anyway), and found it all too loud. I'm an opera fan – though people think this is toffee-nosed!

I should explain that, like many people in Jamaica, I am

mixed-race, half-Chinese. My father was Chinese and my mother is Jamaican, so her blood is mixed as well. My mother was actually brought up by her god-parents, who were English. This mixture presents a certain complication: you are not really Chinese, as you don't speak the language, you haven't got the culture, and you can't therefore really belong to the Chinese community in Jamaica or here. On the other hand, you can't really identify within the West Indian community here either, as in my home life there was much more a mixture of English and Chinese. To many Jamaicans, I do not have a Jamaican outlook at all, and we do not speak the same 'language', by which I mean non-verbal communication. This is what really drove home to me that night.

Of course the further complication, with additional isolating factors, comes in that I'm not really 'at one' with the English, either. I've made a few white English friends, and although I am extremely fond of them, we still do not think along the same lines. There is an unseen barrier. Nevertheless, I find that theirs is the company in which I can more easily relax. The difference between us is so clear, I know I'm not expected to fit in, or be the same. It's a visible difference, too. I don't have to conform to any specific pattern – I can just be myself. As the expression goes: 'Better a stranger in a strange land than a stranger in your own land.' If you change the word 'land' for 'community' then this sums up the situation.

With the English though, you're never entirely relaxed, because racism comes through all the time and in many small ways. You can never be sure of people who at first seem friendly: a man at work was friendly towards me for two or three years, and one evening, because my usual lift wasn't available, I asked him to take me home. He did so the first evening, but the next night, as I waited for him in reception, he said goodnight individually to the other people standing there and walked straight past me out of the door. He never mentioned it to me again – it was ignored, just like that. A similar thing happened later with a woman who I asked for a lift. Like the man, she didn't have the courage to tell me to my face, but later someone told me they'd overheard her saying she didn't want to be seen with a Black person in her car. One soon learns that, although people can be friendly, deep down they are racially prejudiced. One must always remember not to presume friendship, as this presumption often brings out people's true feelings, which usually hurts. So you've got to hold back a little, because you don't want to feel that hurt. Perhaps some of them would like to be good and close friends, but I've learnt never to be sure, and to hold back, which causes further loneliness.

Despite all these things, I don't regret being here. The years of bringing up the children were very hard – low pay, having to work nights to make extra money, struggling to make ends meet, and oh! all the housework. My poor hands were sore from all the washing, because of course we hadn't a machine and I wasn't used to washing clothes anyway. But we coped. Gradually, I met some women at the office who told me that, despite the fact the children were not born here, I was still eligible for family allowance, and a bus driver told us about school travel passes for the children. Donna worked in a factory at first, because she was too young to begin training as a nurse, but eventually she went off to train. Nigel got his 'A' levels, and found he couldn't get into the RAF because of poor hearing, but now he's doing very well indeed, having got an engineering degree. Kerry eventually went to train in youth work, and also has an excellent job.

They've all done so well I feel lucky and proud. This is why I can never regret coming here, as I would not have been able to afford further education for them in Jamaica. Their success means a great deal to me. And I feel very close to them, even if I can't achieve that closeness within other communities here. One daughter lives with me still, and another very near me, and we mean a great deal to each other. My grandchildren are also a great source of pleasure and enjoyment to me.

Although I've been lonely, I haven't for many years thought about remarrying. I'm independent, I enjoy going off visiting different countries on holiday. If I had a husband, I suspect he'd be saying, 'You can't spend all that money on a holiday, we ought to spend it on the house.' I'm used to being able to do what I want, and I couldn't settle into being someone else's wife. In addition to which, who would want to take in any more laundry?

Although I wouldn't want to go back to Jamaica to live, I often dream about it – the night of the full moon, the one you looked forward to because you'd have your beach parties and fires. The time I really miss Jamaican life is at Christmas, which would be open house, nipping over to each others' houses for a drink, and music playing all day long. The two things I would miss back in Jamaica are the opera, and the seasons of the year here – the spring, with the snowdrops and daffodils, the summer, with all the gardens in bloom, and the leaves in autumn. When the snow is on the ground it is just too beautiful for words. The first winter I was here, it was particularly cold one night, and I was sitting on the sofa wrapped in a blanket with my back flat against a radiator. We went to visit a relative, and I sat there, still in my coat and blanket. One of the children came to tell us it was snowing. I forgot how cold it was. I dropped the blanket, I dropped everything, and ran out to play in the snow. I thought I'd never seen anything quite so beautiful. Even now when it snows I like to stand by the window and look out at it for hours.

So life here at the moment is good. I'm still in my job – the salary is not fantastic, but I'm happy with it, and my boss is good. He seems to think I'm superwoman from the amount of work he gives me, but then he works himself just as hard. In six years' time I'll retire, and will find something to do, because the thought of just sitting at home keeping house doesn't appeal to me, since I really dislike housework. Over the next six years, I'll be making my plans on what to do. I've applied for membership of a local golf club and if I'm accepted I'll start my lessons in the summer. I would also like to play bowls and those, along with my present hobbies of cooking and dressmaking will, I think, keep me occupied in retirement.

Meanwhile, I take great pleasure in my children and grandchildren, in their happiness and success, and everything we've achieved together. Now I'm planning my next wonderful holiday – I hope it will be to China. And who knows where after that?

CHAPTER 4

Looking After Three Generations

Vera Carpenter

I took to politics when I was in my late 20s. We lived in a council house on an overspill estate in Harold Hill, built to take in people from the East End of London, where we previously lived. My husband, Harry, was a printer by trade, and already active politically in his union, and in the Communist Party. Some of his interest and involvement rubbed off on me.

While the children were growing up, I was particularly concerned about the unfairness of the education system. Hardly any children on our estate were passing the eleven plus, and I could see how unfair it was to working-class children, what failures it made them feel. It represented much of the unfairness I felt existed in the set-up in this country, and I began to look into political matters. I had to get actively involved myself, and this is how I came to join the Communist Party when I was 29.

I soon became very active and attended branch meetings regularly, making many friends. The branch secretary would come round with his wife to see Harry and me, and out of these many chats I decided to try and set up a women's group. I contacted other women already in the branch – some were in the Party because their husbands were, and others were active in their own right. We met on a weekly basis and discussed women's matters, like child-rearing, money and prices, abortion and birth control. We also took up local issues. For instance, traffic lights or a crossing were needed on the housing estate by the library which had pensioners' housing nearby it. We got up a petition and were interviewed by the local papers and we lobbied the local MP and councillors. We didn't get a crossing but the Ministry of Transport came down and put bollards in instead. We campaigned at a local factory which employed mostly women and wasn't unionised. There were many safety hazards: no first aid and gangways were blocked. We publicised the conditions and though we weren't able to unionise the women at that time, conditions did improve.

We ran jumble sales to make money for the then *Daily Worker* (now the *Morning Star*). These raised money to pay branch dues to the District Committee, and to buy things the branch needed like a typewriter and duplicator. We used to involve the men, but it was all done on the initiative of the women. I took responsibility for the *Daily Worker* Christmas Bazaar which eventually became the second largest to the national one. I'd organise and co-ordinate women to make things. We'd do it together in a group, making toys, clothes, pickling onions – the kitchen in our house would be full of women and children with sacks of pickling onions! From August onwards the house would be loaded from the floor to the ceiling with bazaar goods – you couldn't move.

Afterwards we always felt we had earned a little social. We'd have it at my house, invite the men, and everyone would contribute wine and beer and food. Of course we'd eventually get on to discussing politics – but we used to really enjoy it. It was the only time men came to any of our meetings, unless one was invited to speak on a specific subject.

When I was 32, I was nominated as candidate in the local elections. This meant going out on the knocker every night. Although I wasn't elected, I really enjoyed this – it gave me a chance of meeting different people and I became well known in the neighbourhood. It gave me an insight into other people's concerns. You'd have to treat everyone's problem as if theirs was the only one, and see it as important even if it was trivial. I'd spend a lot of time on the telephone to the council's housing department to insist that repairs were done. Then there were public meetings that I had to speak at. I was nervous, but I knew the majority of people from my canvassing so that helped. Once I'd started talking, I'd pick out one face in the audience and look at that person until I'd warmed up. Then I was elected onto the District Committee and grew much more confident. At that time in my life I would walk into any meeting and say my piece without feeling nervous. Once I was asked to go to a meeting to speak about our women's group to a group of men on strike. I was the only woman to speak at the meeting. Well, I just stood up and said my piece, trying to recruit more women to the group. It went down really well and I was applauded and congratulated. I couldn't have done that before. Working in the women's group gave me a real sense of political confidence.

Later I organised a women's trip to Czechoslovakia. The men had already gone from the print union. I'd had an opportunity to go with Harry, but I didn't fancy leaving the children. So Harry went and took our son Paul who had had severe heart trouble and had been hospitalised for years and had missed out on so much. When they came back I got a report done through some of the women who had been, and I decided to try and get a trip organised especially for our women's group. By the time I suggested it to the women they had their bags packed! We had to widen it outside the group to make up the numbers so we ended up with quite a mixed political group. I advertised in the local paper, and other women's organisations and through CND. In the end we had women from as far away as Dorset and the North East of England. One or two men were critical of it being women only. I argued with them, accusing them of trying to hold women back. I told them that it was all right for them to go to *their* meetings and to the local for their pints as long as their women were at home with their tea on the table and to listen to them spouting on about their politics. Some of the men that I knew were sitting there and squirming in their seats and I said they knew who I was speaking about. They ended up letting their wives go. It's not that my views were unpopular but they often tried to make a joke about it, or ignore what I was saying. I told them they should tear their Party cards up and join the Salvation Army.

Because of the district and national support we were getting, the men ended up doing a turn about. After all, socialism begins at home. Things were such that women and men were really changing and they accepted these changes. Sometimes from now on men would get home from work and the women would be going straight out to a meeting of their own.

But now my own life began to change – strangely in exactly the opposite direction.

A retired doctor who was a Party member lived two doors along. I was the only one he would let into his home to see him. He kept collapsing, and the social services were worried because he wasn't looking after himself. He kept flooding himself out and so on. Because he wouldn't let any home helps in, social services asked me to go in on a daily basis and to be a home help and give him his meals – and to be paid for it! I continued with this almost until he died, but I never considered it a job – I did it because I was fond of him. Meanwhile we were told that my father-in-law couldn't be left on his own any more as he had cancer of the stomach. He wouldn't come and live with us as he wanted to die in his own home. So we moved away from Harold Hill to live with him in Barking. I nursed him for four years – through double incontinence and everything. This took up all of my time, along with my usual care for my husband and children. He was senile and very difficult, and had turned into a horrible man. It was a double strain really because after two years I had to go into hospital myself with cancer of the saliva gland in my neck. In the middle of nursing him I had to look after myself which wasn't easy. At the beginning, even though the journey by bus took over an hour, I used to travel daily back to Harold Hill to look after the doctor and see my friends. One day the doctor was found wandering in the night and he was taken to a geriatric hospital where he died. After that I stopped going over on a daily basis. Although I'm still in contact with some of the women friends there, obviously once the daily contact stopped, I lost much of their support. And with looking after my father-in-law 24 hours a day I couldn't do any political work. I became more or less politically 'dead'.

After three years of looking after my father-in-law, my husband began the first bout of a serious illness (cerebral ischaemia), and was off work for six months. I nursed both of them at once. Six months later my father-in-law died. It was a great relief. What had been so hard was not just the nursing but looking after three generations – father-in-law, husband and adolescent children, with me in the middle trying to keep the peace. Knowing that my father-in-law was so gravely ill, I tried to keep the place as quiet as possible but the children had their lives and needs and that made it difficult and I always felt pulled both ways. But it brought me and Harry closer together – if that was possible, because we were always close. This was because of the size of the problems we were sharing. All through our marriage we shared problems and sorted them out by talking about them until they were sorted out.

By the time my father-in-law died only my youngest daughter, Sue, was still at school. One of my twin daughters, Val, had got married, something it took me a long while to accept, I'm not sure why. But it was the first time I realised she was grown up – a woman. With all the illnesses (mine, Harry's, father-in-law, the doctor) I hadn't noticed. However, with her living just round the corner it wasn't so bad, because I still saw a lot of her.

Shortly after, Harry became much worse. He'd go back to work for a couple of months and then be off sick again. I knew for several years he was going to die. The hospital gave him six months. But he lived much longer. I didn't tell anyone because I wanted his last months to be as normal as possible and if I told anyone they would have treated him differently. With him being so astute he would have realised, but as it was he just thought he had bad circulation of the blood. It was a real strain. On one occasion when he was back at work I went to the local technical college for an interview for a part-time job. I got it, but the next day Harry had a turn for the worse and was taken into hospital. I had to cancel the job as I felt I should be with him all the time. I hadn't been out to work throughout our marriage and I felt I should be with him when he needed me the most.

I decided to tell the children when the turns became more frequent. His behaviour altered to such an extent and he was finding it difficult to cope with things like money and he couldn't go shopping for me any more. I'd got the women in the Co-op to help him and not let on they knew. They'd just pretend they were chatting with him and they'd sort out the money for him. He'd also lose his train of thought in political discussions and say outrageous things. This was terrible for him after all his years of good political work. I didn't want the discussion to stop because he enjoyed them so much and he would have been cut off. It was so difficult to carry on like this, but we had to.

Harry died after three years of illness on and off. Though I'd known he was going to die it was a terrible shock. Every time he went into hospital I'd think, 'Is this the last time?' I thought I'd come to terms with it, but I hadn't. The last time was no different from the other ones. The last evening at home he was in good spirits, laughing and joking with everyone. Then he went ashen and became ill. It was the first time he didn't say to me to leave him alone – he just knew – and I had to help him up the stairs. No one else had seen him like that before and they were all shocked. It had always happened before when we were alone. Only that morning we'd been to the doctor's and he had said that Harry could go back to work in a month – and Harry had said, 'If I'm not in my box by then,' . . . and we walked to the shops hand in hand . . .

Oh, it was such a terrible shock. We'd had such a good

relationship for 24 years. I was 41 when he died, and he was 52. For a while I went on Valium. One day I went to take one and I stopped myself. I just realised I'd end up taking the lot one day or become addicted to them. I thought if he could see me now he wouldn't approve!

Talking now . . . I'm really emotional . . . but it's good for me. It's the first time I've been able to talk about some of these things. We have always been such a close family – talking through everything. Yet we've not been able to talk about Harry in the eleven years since he died. We realise it's something we'll never be able to fully accept or get over.

It felt like I'd lost everything at once. Harry died and the family stopped communicating. Then eight months later Paul got married and three months after that Jacky (Val's twin) got married, and there was just Sue and me at home. Then there was the shock of Val splitting up with her husband only months later! I felt like it was my fault – that since Harry had died I hadn't been able to keep the family together and going. And I've felt the same ever since whenever there have been family problems. I did feel I wanted Paul and Jacky to wait, to hang on and stay with me, but I couldn't and wouldn't say that. It took a lot of strength not to try and stop them – and a couple of days before Paul's wedding I started back on the Valium to get me through.

Six months after Harry died I got my first proper job since marriage – in twenty-four years. It was terrible having to try and get a job. I was so nervous and I'd lost all that confidence I'd built up when I was politically active. Luckily I got a clerical job in a small firm with caring people. I'd not worked in an office since I was 14 – and then in factories in the war – engineering, like in the film *Rosie the Riveter* – until I damaged the tendons in my wrists (it still troubles me). Then I worked in a dyers and cleaners till three months after I got married.

At my interview I told the boss I had been the secretary of a branch of a political party. He asked which party and, though it was a big risk, I told him. Luckily he was interested, being a socialist of sorts himself, and he could see it had given me some sort of relevant experience. Just as well, as I was given a typing test which was awful! I was so nervous and hadn't really done it before. But there was a good atmosphere, and I gave as good as I got from the transport manager – who was also working-class and so shared the same sort of humour. When I heard I'd got the job, starting from 1 p.m. the next day, I felt sick and I didn't even bother trying to go to bed that night. I was so afraid of being late I was ready to go at 10 a.m.! I was on a week's trial and at the end of the week when I was told I'd got the job I was so relieved. Evidently they liked my friendly telephone manner. Within a couple of weeks I'd picked up everything and within three months I was working full-time and running the office. I'd been promoted as secretary to the manager and I had responsibility for supervising the other part-time woman's work. So really the skills and experience I'd picked up in my political work stood me in good stead and I regained confidence in myself.

After four years I met Bill, through work, and found we had a common interest in gardening, and we started seeing each other. At first I felt like a 16-year-old going on my first date. I didn't feel anything for him but it was companionship – not just at the start but all the way through. I needed to fill my time with work and things and companionship was lacking. I never loved Bill and he knew it. Bill was married at the time but he told me his wife was unbearable and they'd not talked for 18 years. I felt sorry for him though I didn't believe *all* the stories. I couldn't understand anyone living all those years like that, given that I'd had such a good marriage. After all Harry and I were very much in love, and we still went into the back row of the pictures and behaved like unmarried teenagers, and we'd go out for a drive down to the lovers' haunts right up until Harry was too ill. We were very fortunate because now I realise that most marriages aren't like that. Harry was always telling me how much he loved me.

Bill's children corroborated most of his stories so I believed him. When he suggested we live together I told him I still loved Harry and would always, and could never love him. We drifted into living together and I remember feeling that it was such a relief not to be having to make all the decisions and have all the worry about the responsibility. But that soon changed and I ended up making the decisions for two. He paid for his keep and I paid for everything else because I wanted to keep my independence and I certainly didn't want to marry, though he did. And there was not much sex with him in six years I was with him. It didn't work out because I was still too much in love with Harry, and I sometimes called him Harry by mistake.

Through this time, living with so many memories of Harry and the past in the same house, I thought it was holding back the relationship with Bill, so I decided to move with him to Devon near my sister. I shouldn't have gone there either because me and Harry had often spoken of getting a smallholding there. I thought I could push the past to the back of my mind, but it was silly, because I couldn't. Things were all right for a while, while Sue was still living with us, but then she moved to Italy and got married and then all the trouble started. Bill turned really nasty and this happened at a time when I felt the loss of my children the worst. Sue was the last to leave and I felt such a loss, a helplessness and hopelessness – I had nothing. Before moving to Devon I had cancer of the other saliva gland again and had another operation and so I was still recovering from this – so all in all I was really down. Of course, when I moved to Devon I left my job and could only get seasonal shop work. After leaving such a good job it was boring and pretty soul-destroying.

Throughout all the time Bill was being obnoxious I got into more of a state and I was close to a breakdown. Bill himself was ill by now. He told me he had cancer. I felt, 'Oh no not again,' and told him that I couldn't nurse him through it. If he had been a different sort of person I would have, but you can't give that much to someone who writes poison pen letters to you and steals from you. I found out anyway that he was lying – he didn't have cancer. I couldn't take any more and eventually told him to go. I could see that his troubles with his wife were his own doing and now I had sympathy for her. I told his children to try and get to know their mother before it was too late, that she probably wasn't the nagger she'd been portrayed. Bill was just a gold digger really, and it was when I told him that there was no more money that he turned on me. When he finally left I felt such relief. I joined night classes and started having some fun with my sister. I started taking students in to make some money and I really enjoyed it. All the time I was in Devon I never saw enough of my children and grandchildren, as the distance stopped us seeing each other. I felt we were all drifting apart. I'd lost confidence again to the extent that I couldn't talk with them – I felt I had nothing to say. What with that and another illness recurring (Jorgens Syndrome) my doctor advised me to move back to Essex to be closer to my children. I'd got a lot from Devon though – a tranquillity I'd not known before from the sea and countryside, and the slower pace of life and getting involved in my nephew's school for retarded children. The involvement in the school was good for me – I felt I was doing some good for someone and that I was needed.

When I first saw the bungalow in Southend, I knew it was for me. The bedroom was decorated in the same colours – an unusual combination – that mine and Harry's was done in, and there were other signs that made me feel it was the place to settle. Since moving back I've been very ill again with blood and bowel complaints and it's felt very uphill. I've not been able to look for a job – even if there was one to get these days. And I've been housebound a lot and my doctor is trying to get me invalidity benefit. I feel as though I'm in mid-air, not knowing what I can do. Of course a widow's pension would be a joke if it wasn't so pitiful, and my savings have fast dwindled over the years. I'm really restricted. When you become a widow you're told to start a new life, but people don't know how hard it is. You're told to join clubs, that costs money and it feels a bit like putting myself onto some sort of cattle market. Men or younger women can go to a pub for a drink, but a woman my age couldn't do that. People think you're on the pick-up. You can't just go out and make a new social life. I see my children and old friends more now, but in the course of an average day I'm completely cut off – so it's harder to converse with people than it ever was. Though I'm doing things in the house I'm not confident about it. However, I'm pleased and proud of the things I've learnt to do, like difficult decorating.

I just don't have the opportunities to have contact with people outside my family. I'm hoping that when I'm in better health I'll be able to join night classes again. So unless I can get a job, the only way I can make a social life is to do some voluntary work or political work – but then again that is going to cost me more money than I can afford. So life seems a bit directionless at the moment. I realise I can still make changes – and that I alone can make them. I need to find the confidence to meet the challenge once again.

CHAPTER 5

Turning Points – Into the Women's Movement

Jan Russell

I came to England from New Zealand in 1958 when I was 22. After various jobs in offices, waitressing, and in a hospital, I met my husband, and we married when I was 25. In the first few years of our marriage, my husband did labouring and factory work. We lived with two children in one room, and money was very short. He was often laid off, leaving us in pretty desperate straits. We decided to move to one of the London overspill council estates in Luton, which would be a solution to our housing problem, and provide better job prospects for him. He got work 'on the track' at the Vauxhall car factory. But this, too, was never constant – he would often be put on short time. We also felt that he could do something more satisfying that might bring in a more secure income too. After three years 'on the track' he began a course to train to be a teacher, as a mature student. We now had a third child, and their ages were 2, 5 and 7.

I'd encouraged him to go to college, but I can remember thinking that I was capable of doing so myself. So I envied him quite a bit, especially as I had to take even more responsibility in looking after the children, as his studying spilled over into the evenings. Because he was on a student grant, this was a very penniless phase for us again. During his second year, around Christmas, a new worry entered my life when my middle child, a boy, developed epilepsy, something I had myself in my 20s. He took about five years to get better from it, though it disappeared eventually as suddenly as it had begun, just as it did with me.

All this time I remained at home to care for the children, but during my husband's final year, when my youngest was coming up to school age, I returned to work. I went part-time at first, as a receptionist and clerical officer in a local hospital, and this somewhat alleviated our money troubles.

Around this time a new problem arose. Just as my husband's course was nearing an end, I got pregnant. I was on the pill, but I had been ill with a bout of food-poisoning, and although I didn't think about it at the time, of course the pill had gone out of my system. Naturally at first I was astounded to find myself pregnant, and then very worried. I knew that I didn't want any more children, and that I wanted to have an abortion, but I didn't know quite how to go about it. I went to the doctor to ask her, but she told me she thought I could cope with another child. When I became distressed she said she thought I didn't know my own mind, and that I'd feel better about it in a few days. She was sure, she said, that my husband would support me through it. Whatever I said to her, she blocked off, showing no understanding of what it's like not to have any money, not to want to bring any more children into that situation, and to want to start on a new job myself – all the things thousands of mothers who've been confined with small children much of the time know only too well.

I went back to the evening surgery with my husband, but she still didn't believe that we could want an abortion. Two days later we went back again, and this time saw one of the male partners. By this time I was even more distressed, but he was equally obstructive, and told us he wouldn't recommend us for an NHS abortion. My husband ended up having a row with him, to which his response was that we should find another practice.

I'd also been to my Family Planning clinic, where the doctor had been sympathetic, and had obviously tried to discuss it with my own GP, all to no avail. In the end, the only way we could get around it was for my husband to stand in the phone box ringing round all the London teaching hospitals until somebody referred us to a private consultant. This meant money which we didn't have, so we borrowed it from friends. Even today I have not recovered from the anger I feel about the ordeal I went through at the hands of those doctors, and how it all boils down to who has got the money.

Over the years that followed I remained in work, putting all my earnings into the house and children. I went to night school and took English 'O' level, and after I left the job at the hospital, I went to work in a doctor's surgery. I then left, and took a full time TOPS typing course. All this helped me to get a post as a clerical officer in adult education, bringing me into contact with a lot of women tutors working part-time. I found them very stimulating, and this reinforced the sense that I had within me more than I was bringing out.

I began to see further education as a real possibility. Here were women who were bringing up young children, but also working in worthwhile and demanding jobs. They also had strong opinions about how they should be allowed to express themselves in their own work and were confident that they had that right equally with their husbands. They didn't, I think, identify themselves as feminists at that stage (the mid 1970s) and nor had I, yet, come into contact with feminism as such. If you're living on a big council estate, there isn't much opportunity to come into contact with feminists, in terms of meetings and discussions, since most of the women were up really early getting their families off, then out to work themselves, and back again later looking after their families through the evenings.

Looking back on my work there, I know it to have been an important turning point for me. First the contact with the women tutors, then the fact that I had enormous responsibilities, usually the only person in the office doing all the administration. This all led to my becoming more involved with my work there, especially as the adult literacy scheme grew, increasing the scope of my job. One advantage to having a teacher as a husband is that I could work through the holidays, with him at home for the children.

I began to feel the need to make changes, but I couldn't yet see clearly how they could ever happen. I felt frustrated at how to make anything come about. My husband seemed content enough with the way things were, and I couldn't express my unhappiness because I wasn't yet clear about why I felt as I did. At the time, too, all our friends assumed that we were a happy, complete, stable nuclear family. Perhaps, too, I felt reluctant to take the initiative in making changes when I did not feel ready to take responsibility for the consequences which might follow.

But for all my tentativeness and confusion, what grew was my awareness of my role as a woman. A key point of change was my struggle – on my own because I was the only worker there on that grade – to be regraded. I belonged to the union, and I was very aware that most workers on this low grade were women. Another catalyst for me was the fight against the Corrie Anti-Abortion Bill during the late 1970s. All the humiliation I'd been put through only a few years earlier was still at the forefront of my memory, and I just can't adequately express the great concern I felt that this bill might get through. I was very determined that this time I wasn't going to stand back, but that I would try to do something to prevent it being passed.

I asked a woman I'd met at work if she knew of any groups organising against the bill. It turned out that she was involved herself, and this is how I got involved in my first women's group. About six of us met every week to discuss ways of organising against Corrie. We also talked about many aspects of women's lives – especially their expected role as mothers. At last I felt able, with these women, to express my opinions. It was the first time in my life that I felt that what I had to say was valid. Always before I'd felt that people discounted my ideas, but in this group women listened to me, taking up the points I made, whether they agreed or not. I still remember it for the warmth I felt there, feeling comfortable in a way I hadn't ever before.

As I talked and listened in this group, I began to get insights into the ways in which I was myself conforming to things I didn't believe in, understanding how perhaps I was afraid to break out, and also the pressure on women to stay within these patterns.

And yet I still didn't *really* believe it was seriously possible that I could make a life of my own. I was still in the marriage physically, if not mentally, and couldn't see any way out of it yet. Now I was beginning to meet women, both lesbian and heterosexual, who *were* living lives different from the patterns expected of women. And gradually I came to see it wasn't just a dream.

It could happen. This made me acknowledge my own lesbian feelings which over many years I'd been afraid to express. I'd kept on concealing them even though I'd felt very strongly for several women friends over the past few years. Since we were all married, none of us dared to discuss it. I dealt with it (and perhaps they did) by feeling it was just me, being 'immature'. Meeting women who were living openly as lesbian feminists gave me new perspectives and new hope.

I felt real relief at the defeat of the Corrie Bill, and elation that I'd taken part in something successful. Some of us decided we'd now try to work towards setting up a Rape Crisis Centre in Luton. I also started going to women's conferences and events, gradually finding myself more and more involved in the women's movement.

My husband felt resentful that I was going off to things he couldn't attend. He sensed I was becoming more independent, and that in many ways I was leaving him behind. The strain in my marriage began to grow with my feelings that I needed to make radical changes. I could no longer suppress the feelings of affection and commitment I'd felt for women for so long, right back to my school days. One night I arrived home to find him in quite a state. He said he really wanted to know what was happening and I told him that I'd try to remain in the marriage for another year, to give us both time to sort things out, but that I had decided I could not stay indefinitely, and that I was a lesbian. Over the next few weeks, although we tried it was impossible for us to have any real discussions about it. He'd start off being understanding but quickly turn hostile. He blamed what was happening on my involvement in the women's movement, and he also thought we could make it possible for me to stay in the marriage and be a lesbian. Of course I'm aware that many women do choose this option, but I couldn't possibly have stayed in an outwardly conventional marriage the way my politics were developing. I just couldn't myself have led two lives.

Within a couple of months, with the stress of it all no doubt, I fell quite ill with a serious viral infection. He looked after me, and I felt very guilty about the pain I was inflicting on him. My children sensed that something was going on. I decided to tell my eldest, my daughter, who was now 18. She was fairly interested in feminism herself, so I thought she would understand some of it. She was very supportive and told me she'd been thinking anyway I might now be a lesbian, and of course I was very relieved.

When I recovered, I decided to leave my job to give myself the time to find the right educational avenue, as I knew I wanted to study, and could see this was one important way out of my situation. Friends strongly advised me to get into university as a mature student, but I lacked the confidence to do so. Then another told me about Hillcroft College. This is a women's residential college for adult education, where you can take various courses, and, if you want, go on to university. It is possible to get in without having 'O' and 'A' levels. If you gain a place there, you automatically receive a grant. It seemed exactly right for me and so everything fell into place.

I applied, and was accepted for the coming September. In the few months before term started, the assumption at home was that I'd still be back home in all the holidays and I thought that too. After all, I had nowhere else to go, and no income except my grant, which was, in any case, subject to my husband's earnings, and therefore very small. And I felt guilty about not being a proper mother. At first I went home every other weekend – and found myself doing all the housework, an expression of my guilty feelings. My husband was hostile. The course demanded a lot of work. So what with one thing and another, I came to realise that they could manage without me (my youngest was now 14) and gradually my term-time visits became more sporadic.

Although Hillcroft undoubtedly gave me the opportunity I needed to leave home and take up further education, I did find it hard going most of the time. It was a very intensive course and the first time I'd undertaken any academic work, apart from my English 'O' level, since leaving school at 15. Many women had problems, both academic and personal – something common to quite a few of us was husbands and children not being able to come to terms with our increasing independence, and, of course, not being able to cope so comfortably without us there servicing them. Some of the married women there were under stress because of family conflict, and several of us, in addition, felt we weren't up to standard on the courses. More counselling services there would certainly be an improvement – but most of us still battled through and are now doing what we wanted. Some of my year group went on to university, some into jobs. It's a unique college in that it offers to women an opportunity learn and study with other women. There are now also some short courses held at the college.

Despite all my husband's protestations about me being the only one for him, within a few months of my being in college, he had met another woman and soon began divorce proceedings. Earlier, in my women's group, I'd gone through the guilty feelings I had about leaving him, and they'd all told me, 'Don't worry, within a year he'll find someone else,' but of course I hadn't believed them. Meanwhile I was still trying to manage on a small grant, and realising what I'd done by putting all the years of money I'd earned into the household, never any into savings for myself, never having my own separate account. By the time the divorce came through I had virtually finished the course, so my income while there never increased. Nor was I ever to get anything like my own 'share' of money back from the past years together, and the eventual settlement was tiny.

During my last year at Hillcroft I wanted to live out of college and found a small room through a housing association – the first time in my life I'd ever lived on my own! It really dawned on me then how penniless women are in my situation, and how it's often the thought of poverty and discomfort that must keep so many from making the decision to leave their marriages.

I was lonely and depressed, worrying about money and about the course and the approaching assessments. But I was still meeting women who supported and helped me. Around this time I joined the Older Feminist Network, and at times of great stress and panic several of my friends saw me through. It is very important that women help each other through these stressful times of change. It would have been impossible for me to survive everything without my various women's groups during those years.

When you're older you tend to think it's more difficult to make changes, but looking back, I'm only surprised that I didn't do it sooner! I feel fairly settled now. I've moved into a house where I am happily sharing with a feminist friend, but I'm pleased that first I learnt to live on my own. I qualified from Hillcroft, but decided not to go on further with education for the present as I want to work. I've been reasonably successful in finding temporary work, but I hope eventually to be able to work in the community where I live, and also in the field I'm interested in: working with women. I've now joined the collective of the local

Women's Centre, where I did my placement in my final college year.

I'm close to my daughter, and my sons are getting along all right. I feel that at last I'm beginning to live my life on my own terms. Of course working on this piece had made me realise that all the anger, guilt and pain you keep down inside you over the years doesn't just go away. I can feel it there still, and it still wells to the surface and upsets me. But now I realise how change comes out of these feelings, pushes you on, and remains a part of you – and, in my case, forges a strong link with other women which will last inside me and guide what I do from now on.

It seems a long time ago since I left home, and I feel very distant from that time now. Lately I've been thinking I'd like to go back to New Zealand for a holiday. I haven't been back there since I left as a very young woman. I can feel myself becoming more interested in the place of my childhood and youth and wanting to see what's happening politically in New Zealand. I wonder how my family will receive me!

CHAPTER 6

Recovering from 'Religion'

Ann Gabriel

I started teaching in Scotland when I was 22. My brother and sister had left home in their late teens, and my mother was completely financially dependent on me. I felt I just had to stay with her. Although I provided the finance my mother made all the decisions. She was the voice of authority, though never a strident voice, and I obeyed without question. My leisure time was organised by her too, and I also accepted this. As the years passed I began to feel trapped in this caring financial relationship. However, I gave her no outward sign of my feelings.

Now and again a man would show some interest in me, and I would tell him, 'If you want to marry me, you'll have to marry my mother as well.' Of course they all felt unable to take on such a problem. At the time I was not devastated by these rejections. I had been taught that self-sacrifice would be very highly rewarded in the next life. I firmly believed it.

The early religious indoctrination and intimidation I'd received was so thorough that I lived most of my life in a state of fear. Everything was a sin, even thinking, or most of all thinking. As a result I'd developed a habit of lying about even the most trivial things, especially to avoid the slightest punishment or blame.

Eventually I met Michael. My position with regard to my mother remained the same and I explained this to him. But this time I received the reply, 'We'll tackle the problem together', and we did. I was so pleased for someone else to make the decisions, as my religious training tended to make me want to leave such matters to others. Then started a marvellous transformation in my life. I saw Michael's tolerance, his confidence, his caring and it began to rub off on to me. I soon realised that my life up until then had been a nothing, a non-thinking obedience, a fear of authority colouring it all. On reflection, I shudder to think how I would have behaved if I had been exposed to a Hitler-like regime before I met Michael. Now at last I began to feel alive.

But I still had difficulty with the habit of lying to protect myself, always imagining the awful punishments I would incur if I was less than perfect. Once when I told Michael a lie I remember him asking, 'Ann, what are you afraid of? Have I ever done or said anything to make you afraid of me?' He was upset, judging my lying to be a sign that I lacked confidence in him. It took him a long while to understand its real source: the steady religious indoctrination from my earliest years at school, the repetition day after day, from the age of seven: 'Those who die in mortal sin, will go to hell for all eternity.' It was explained to us that hell was a place where you burned, and that 'all eternity' meant that the burning went on and on and on. I remember so well feeling terrified. With a doctrine like this I am now not surprised at the burning of millions of witches over a period of 300 years. In the minds of the fathers of the church, this was as nothing compared to the torment of hell forever.

This indoctrination continued until I was 18, and it led me to believe in a vindictive male God who really didn't think much of women, but wanted us to be docile, submissive and non-thinking.

Quite recently I have made a study of the Gospels, but not selectively, and there I found, even to my surprise, ample evidence of this vengeful God's attitude toward those who are not meek and mild enough to believe everything He said (or is supposed to have said). If they do not, punishment without mercy!

When Michael realised how pervasive these ideas were within my past, he also realised how deeply ran my lack of self-confidence. Gradually as the years passed I stopped lying. I began slowly to feel more secure, more able to express an opinion, and more self-confident. Michael remained consistently supportive. Once when the headmistress where I worked wanted to push me out to another school in order to accommodate a teacher friend of hers, I said, 'Yes, yes, of course,' when all the while I did not want to leave at all, and the new school would have been entirely inconvenient for me. Yet I was too terrified of the voice of authority to say so. When Michael heard about this he asked me if I really wanted to teach in the other school, and I told him I didn't. He came with me to see the headmistress, and told her, quite correctly, that she had no authority to transfer me. And thus it was settled that I didn't have to go. At the time I thought how very much I would have liked to have been able to do this for myself. I couldn't.

I came to lean on Michael. He was strong and good, and exposed to his influence I, too, became stronger. At least I thought I had genuinely imbibed his strength. Then suddenly he died. I felt absolutely incapable of coping with the situation. The only way I could go on was to think about our 9-year-old daughter, Susan. I had to stay alive for her. But, at the time, strangely, I found it very hard to be with her, because I suppose she reminded me so painfully and vividly of her father. So, although she went on living with me, to all outward appearances, with me going through all the motions of being a good and reliable mother, I'd arrange for friends to pick her up after school, and keep her for tea or sometimes overnight with their children. I looked for holidays which she could go off on without me. For a year I remained in this state, just getting through the days somehow, being always caring of Susan, but emotionally holding her off. I returned to the state of trying not to think, which, because of all my training, was only too easy to slip back into.

About a year later friends introduced me to John, who was not only kind to me, but also took a kindly interest in Susan. After a very short period I married him. I now recognise that I was in a state of desperation to get out of my sense of being lost, and that I was suffering from a strong feeling that I was absolutely incapable of bringing up one small girl as her father would have done. I felt completely inadequate, convinced I couldn't manage it alone. I thought also I would get back the aliveness that I had experienced with Michael.

After a short while John's behaviour towards us both began to change. He too had been raised as a Catholic, and the teachings of his childhood began to assert themselves over Susan and me. He followed his beliefs in everlasting punishment. He was never physically violent: *his* method of punishment was silence, something he exerted if I didn't agree with every word he said, on every topic, no matter how silly or prejudiced. I was really terrified of these silences, so I very soon started to placate him in every way I could think of. I bribed him with the little money that Michael had left me. No doubt I ought to have kept this for Susan. I didn't. She could do with it now. I kept praising him continually in the hope that this might make him stop the dreadful silences. At first they lasted hours, then as time went on, weeks, and finally months. This was more than I could stand so I regressed again to telling lies for fear of this treatment.

For Susan it was even worse. She was entering adolescence, and his psychological brutality had terrible effects. She would return home from school every day to find him ignoring her when she spoke, turning his head away, never looking at her. She developed anorexia, and skin trouble. There then followed a long and difficult period for both Susan and me, and I began to realise just how seriously affected she'd been by the events of the past years, and that John could not be allowed to go on exerting his cruelty over her.

I realise that he was a victim of the evil teachings of his church, and that he no doubt felt justified in his punishment techniques. After all, he'd been taught 'believe me or else' and that's the way he himself behaved towards Susan and me. I'd had enough; somehow I found the strength and courage to make him leave.

Although at last I'd taken some action on my own and Susan's account, I still found it difficult to assert myself in my work. I was still teaching, and often found myself holding very different ideas from the other teachers. Yet I could not bring myself to express my opinions at our open staff meetings. I noticed that the only other Roman Catholic on the staff also said nothing on such occasions. Just about this time Susan herself went to university, and then on to train as a teacher. Through reading some of her progressive books on education and discussing these ideas with her, I began slowly to change.

I'd begun to suspect that children should not be disciplined in some of the more conventional ways, like carrots and sticks for individual achievements, gold stars and so on, and these discussions with Susan confirmed my views. I had a reception class, the youngest infants, and I decided to change the way I controlled them, to do away with all such kinds of rewards and punishments. Eventually, over a period of time, the rest of the school changed too. They could see how the changes I'd made brought me closer to the children.

Because my new methods aimed at inspiring a love of learning, their achievements grew by leaps and bounds.

Despite all these changes and my influence there, I had several deep differences with the other teachers, especially over such matters as religion, in which my colleagues were either conventionally wishy-washy, sticking to traditional kinds of propaganda, or openly and strongly pushing the Bible. Yet I could not argue these matters out at staff meetings, and continued to lack the necessary confidence to do so. I began to think that since I was evidently not improving in this respect perhaps I should retire early and try to do something really positive about becoming more assertive, less dependent, and more generally confident in myself.

So at 55 I came to make the decision to retire, but strangely with no real idea of what I was going to do. What followed came as much as a surprise to me as it did to my friends. I retired at more or less the same time that Susan, now finished her training, went to London to live. She was becoming more and more interested in radical feminism. Our discussions continued, and I found myself very interested for the first time in my life in something that seemed to me to be entirely positive: women not depending on someone else's approval, or someone else's decisions, but living and working together to support each other in developing each other's strengths as well as our own. As the months passed my relationship with Susan began to change again. She did not try to influence me, but just by her being herself I began truly to realise all that I owed her from the past. For me, feeling close again to her and her ideas brought me great joy, one that has gone on growing, a deeper joy than I have ever known before in my whole life.

I began to read about feminism, devouring many books on many aspects of the women's movement, and to be active in it by joining women's groups and going to discussions. I also joined a local group of humanists, and was delighted to find that they have an attitude to life which I can adopt wholeheartedly, with its abhorrence of all forms of fanaticism, all sexual and racial discrimination, and with its belief that any progress towards a better life for all, any improvement in the quality of life for all, necessitates a continuing committed *human* effort. They do not believe in the intrusive tyrannies of religions which for so many centuries in the past ruled men, women and children in their thoughts, emotions, choices and actions. On the contrary, for centuries humanism has upheld a belief in the ideal of the individual as the right and proper source of her/his actions, guided by the supremely human faculties of reason and imagination, and imbued with a love full of understanding and respect. Humanists believe that there is a future for womankind and mankind and that the proper saviour of the human race is not some mythical, all-powerful, vengeful being, but the human race itself.

After some time I was able for the first time in my life to express openly the anger I felt at the damage done to me by the male cult of Christianity. Through meetings with my humanist friends I have started to work out my own deep beliefs and reject those imposed on me by religious indoctrination. I have begun to uncover my caring and rational side, which was so systematically trained out of me as a child.

At last, in my wonderful new relationship with my daughter, and through the interest and bond I feel with her in our commitment to women through feminism, along with the forging of a new set of wide beliefs, I seem to be able, suddenly, to be me.

The terrible dependency I had is diminishing. I am looking forward eagerly to being able to accept myself, body and mind, as a complete, powerful and strong human being. I know now that nothing and nobody can reverse my progress. I'm glad I retired, as my life since then has been so full. An everyday awareness is growing where before it didn't exist, or had been dampened down. I know fully now that I am not just somebody's daughter, sister, wife or mother, living vicariously through other people. I am sure that life can be lived independently, wholeheartedly and joyfully. This is its meaning and purpose.

For me, this is the beginning of my new life – a real happiness.

CHAPTER 7

From Assimilation to Identity

Leah Shaw

I was born in Germany in 1919 into an assimilated and quite right-wing Jewish family. My parents were divorced very soon after I was born, and my mother took me back to live with her parents whose very German, assimilant and yet religiously Jewish attitudes were very significant for me when I was little.

I was 14 when Hitler came to power in Germany. It was clear I could not stay at the German school I attended, so I moved to a Jewish school in the country. Here the atmosphere was wonderfully stimulating, both on an intellectual and personal level. I became very religious – the school was permeated by the ideas of Martin Buber. Later I moved to Berlin, where I lived in the house of another assimilated but left-wing family. Here again I learnt a great deal, mainly about socialism. This extraordinary couple died in the gas chamber during the war.

While I was studying in Berlin in preparation for the English school certificate I met a young man who had an entry certificate to Palestine. We contracted a fictitious marriage, and that is how I got out of Germany and into Palestine in 1938. While I was there, in 1940, all the Jews in our area of Germany, Baden, were picked up one night, my mother among them, and transported to a concentration camp in the South of France. Conditions there were very hard, and my mother died in the camp. My grandmother died from neglect in a hospital after her flat had been taken from her by the state.

During my first year in Palestine I lived in a kibbutz, then moved to Jerusalem where I trained as a nurse. Because I knew English well, I used to enjoy the company of English people and never really became part of the Jewish community. I think I was having another go at assimilation: having been an assimilated Jewish woman in Germany, I was once again undergoing the same process. When Hitler had come to power, we had all become very Jewish. It was a natural reaction. I became Zionist and wanted very much to go to Palestine. Once there I became aware of all the contradictions, of being Jewish and the position of the Arabs, of trying to live out socialist beliefs and the political realities of Palestine.

After going out with an Englishman for several years, I met a British soldier who happened to be Jewish. When he was transferred to Egypt we corresponded (I still have all the letters) and on his return to Jerusalem we got married. That was in 1944, and the following January he was repatriated: that is how I came to arrive in wartime England on a troop ship. Louis and I did not know each other very well: the ambience in Jerusalem was very different from that in London. Basically I had got married in a desperate search for security, which of course I now know to be an illusion. We did have something intellectual in common, like the love of reading, but I was not in sympathy with his desire, once he got back here, to give up his profession as a draughtsman and go into business. The Jewish petty bourgeois ideal of 'having your own business' prevalent in his family really got a hold on him, and because I did not agree with that, it caused a lot of trouble between us. However, at that time I did not have enough knowledge of the country to give my feelings power. He had already bought a radio business while in the army, and later went into the furniture business with his father and brother, but he was never a businessman really.

I did not tell anyone here I was a nurse, because becoming a nurse had been entirely wrong for me. What I really wanted to do was to become a librarian, but first I needed to try to obtain my school certificate which I'd had to drop when I left Germany. Because I was working part-time, and then became pregnant, I could not really manage this, although I did work part-time for some years in public libraries.

During the early years of our marriage we lived in Brixton, after having stayed with my husband's parents in Hackney. There had been tension with my mother-in-law, who felt I was showing off with my middle-class origins which she resented. She was working-class but with bourgeois values, very concerned with 'good manners', not talking to your neighbours and so on. The last thing I wanted to be was like that. In Brixton I did not know anybody and was completely isolated and unhappy. We had difficulties in our marriage, partly because I considered myself more cultured and intelligent than my husband, which I now see as false. In spite of our many difficulties, many of them due to me, I often think I would still be able to live with my husband, because I have met a number of men since his death, and when I compare them he was not so bad. After he died, I heard that during his last year he had been involved with another woman. The woman herself told me.

I had my two older children one after another and went through a terrible period. Then I got pregnant again and to get a legal abortion I had to fake a mental breakdown, though I was in fact mentally distressed. Later I had another abortion, with my husband being in agreement both times. I never really wanted any children. It happened to me without my having chosen it. I don't think I love children *per se*, whether mine or someone else's. Young children make me anxious and this is how I feel about my son's children even today. Louis was a wonderful father. He was a much better parent than I was, with a warmth and enjoyment in the children that I did not have. He had the right attitude when they were young, but when they started growing up – when my eldest daughter started going out with boys — he became very authoritarian. We had different attitudes towards sex between young people. I thought they should be allowed to do what they wanted, and in their own homes. He was not in agreement. He died when my youngest daughter was 13, we were both 38, and the other two were at university.

After our early years in Brixton, where I had felt so lonely, we moved to Northolt. The children started school and I started meeting people, suburban friends. Somehow we slipped into suburban life. Then we moved to Birmingham where I got more interested in becoming politically active. I joined the Labour Party and was active in the early CND campaigns. I took a secretarial course there when I was 42, and worked in industry as a secretary. We had moved to Birmingham so that Louis could go back to being a draughtsman/designer, and at last he became a reliable money-earner. He had wanted me to do something more worthwhile, like teaching, but I had not wanted to do that. So I ended up doing something quite low-grade because I did not have the confidence to do anything more demanding. I soon realised I did not like working in industry and tried to get a job at the university as a secretary. I was not successful immediately, then Louis died and, going again for security – job security this time – I remained in my job in the car industry. I was there in all for 19 years, until early, and forced, retirement.

I think my husband actively avoided any reference to being Jewish. We led a Jewish life without being very Jewish. I myself was, and still am, very anti-religious, and to me Judaism is connected with religion. Since I could not pass on any religion to my children, I did not pass on much Judaism, except what I was myself. I did not say, 'I am not Jewish.' If one is Jewish, one does not 'grow out of it' at a particular time. After the war, because of the things that had happened, you really thought you were finished with anti-semitism. It is through the growth of post-war anti-semitism that you are forced to confront this again. While I am quite ambivalent about what it means to be

Jewish, I am not at all ambivalent about fighting the growing racism in our society.

After my husband died, I very much wanted to get married again – security! I had several relationships and was once very much in love. But I could not see any of these relationships as becoming useful or permanent. Nor has the sexual side of relationships with men ever been very good or important to me. At that time I became interested in feminism and this took me away from the desperate urge of looking for someone. It was a great relief to realise I did not need relationships with men to be reasonably contented. That was not the reason I became a feminist, but it was one of the spin-offs.

Feminism was in the air at the time, 1969-70. I first became interested through reading *The Female Eunuch*. I picked up this interest independently of my daughters, developing it also through a women's history course I attended in adult education for a number of years. I was then in my 50s, and became involved in the women's liberation movement in Birmingham – I went to meetings, conferences, demos, was active in WARF (Women Against Racism and Fascism) and also part of the co-ordinating group organising the last of the National Women's Liberation Conferences, which was held in Birmingham in 1978. But really I always felt quite peripheral to the whole scene. I was friendly with one particular woman who used to involve me in everything, but when that friendship ended, my involvement with the movement almost came to an end. There were very few other older women involved, and I also lived some way out of Birmingham, which did not help. In my experience, the women's liberation movement is not very good at holding women together.

My intention now is to be more involved with local groups, whether they are specifically feminist or not. For example, I am involved in local CND, which is not specifically a women's group. Meanwhile I have met quite a number of nice women where I live and we have actually got a women's group together in this very suburban area. It is intended to be a consciousness-raising group and even though I am the oldest there, I don't feel so peripheral. In those earlier days I felt that the women who *were* the women's liberation movement in Birmingham were all high-powered intellectuals, either university lecturers or working at the Centre for Cultural Studies, doing PhDs and women's studies. I admired them all, but could not really keep up with them. Also they were all much younger than me. I met up with one of these women more recently, when some of us went to Greenham Common. She was dishing out papers to foreign women to explain their legal rights in case they were arrested and she said to me, 'Ach, you are Israeli, aren't you?' I replied, 'How can you ask me this when I've known you for so long?' I felt it was anti-semitic of her to show such a lack of knowledge of someone she had known for years and been in groups with.

My two daughters have encouraged me to take more interest in my Jewish identity; they value my knowledge of Jewish matters, and naturally when there is a demand one is willing to communicate information. My eldest daughter was living in the USA, and became very Jewish-identified many years ago, studying Yiddish, mixing with only Jewish women. Then my younger daughter became involved in Jewish feminism, and I attended the first national Jewish Feminist Conference in London in 1981. At the time of the Israeli attack on Lebanon in 1982 some Jewish feminists in Birmingham got together for mutual support. This happened at the same time that the two feminist publications, *Spare Rib* magazine and *Outwrite* newspaper, started printing articles that many Jewish women experienced as anti-semitic. We started reading widely and prepared a talk for a women's liberation day conference stressing how the situation in Israel had arisen. For a short time I also attended meetings of a semitic women's group and a mixed (men and women) Arab/Jewish group. But I always have trouble when the line of argument is unquestioningly Palestinian. The way the problems of Israelis/Palestinians are talked about today leaves out past developments. For instance, it's always the Israelis who are seen as aggressive, when Arabs have been just as aggressive in the past. Of course, it is very upsetting to hear about the nature of Israeli military government on the West Bank and similar matters. In spite of the knowledge that Israel is acting in some disastrous ways at the moment, I am defensive about Israel, because I can't forget that if it hadn't been for the possibility of going to Palestine, I would not be alive today. It was also Zionism – the wish to go to Palestine – that helped me to survive in the Nazi environment. It gave me an identity I don't want to disassociate myself from, even if I can't identify with military governments. I have never been back since I left Palestine in 1945. We have a Jewish feminist group in Birmingham which I find very supportive.

At one time, when the children were very young, my husband wanted us to go and live in Israel. I did not want to go, partly because of my uneasiness with regard to the whole situation there, but also because in 1945, when the Labour government came to power, there was such a wonderful atmosphere of hope in this country, with the creation of the health service, the educational system and so on. Nowadays I see all the progressive movements being choked by the forces of reaction. I am not a revolutionary, because I think revolution is too quick a way of bringing about necessary changes of consciousness and therefore carries its own seeds of failure. Now that all those hopeful structures established in the late 1940s are being destroyed, it is hard for me to see this failure of an evolutionary process, and yet still not be able to come down completely on the side of revolution. In this country now you don't feel that anyone looks after your health and you feel forsaken. It's a very real fear for older people, falling ill, especially when your children are far away, leading their own lives.

I don't see the prospect of many radical changes taking place, because of the very entrenched positions of the powers which run our lives. I see that we ought to live entirely differently in the ways we group together and in the ways we get our emotional security and warmth. Although I did like kibbutz communal life, my ideas today are far more revolutionary with regard to the kind of society I should like to see develop than when I was living in the kibbutz. For instance, it is true we did not care whether we were legally married, but the stress was nevertheless on 'permanent' monogamous heterosexual relationships, and in those days I always used to want the company of men, and I would always talk to them in any group, and not to the women. Now I seek out the company of women more and feel closer to women than men. The position of women is being encroached upon all the time by this government – something that is happening all over the world.

The human being I feel closest to is my younger daughter: she gives me a lot of emotional warmth. I have also learnt a lot from her; both my daughters have enriched my life a great deal, intellectually and emotionally. They both became lesbians and I did not have any difficulty in accepting the validity of their thoughts and ideas. The book *Sappho Was a Right On Woman* opened my eyes to a whole different world, a very acceptable world in my eyes. As for my son, I was very close to him when he was young, but I had a lot of trouble identifying with a very spiritual/religious phase he went through. And because his ideas about feminism are absolutely false, there is a gap of understanding, but we have a very loving relationship.

As for me, sexually I'm very much in abeyance. I think that today if any kind of emotional experience came my way I would very happily accept it. I don't expect it and I don't hope for it. I would love it to happen to me, but it is the kind of longing that I don't think will be fulfilled. A lot of my efforts are now devoted to working for CND. I think the fight against nuclear weapons is a very important one. And though sometimes I sink into feeling we can't achieve very much – and anyway, is the human race *worth* saving – I do what I can.

CHAPTER 8

Claiming a Self – Insights from a Complex Marriage

Marjorie Duncan Lawrie

I was married at 18 – and plunged into it with enthusiasm. But after about three years I realised I had missed quite a lot, especially as I knew I'd been capable of going to university. My husband was considerably older than me, and played a tutoring role – he believed that I could learn most of what I needed from him. Indeed, he did teach me a tremendous amount, sharing all his thoughts and ideas with me in a marvellous way. He was a lecturer and later a journalist, and I did all his typing. But I felt on the circumference of things. I wanted to contribute something of my own. I remember that when I was about 20 I came across this in a newspaper: 'What does a woman have to live for after 40?' I was aware that before I reached that age my children would be off my hands. I decided that I would train.

As it happened, I was exactly 40 when my husband stopped freelancing from home and started to work full-time in London, which meant that he stayed there several days each week. I could see that this was a good time for me to begin training, and I decided on social studies. I can remember the exact spot I was standing in the garden when I realised that, with my husband now away from home, and my part in his work so reduced, I was completely on the outside of things. Totally unexpectedly, I found that I couldn't breathe. Trying to mow the grass, I didn't understand what was wrong – but I had developed asthma. Over the next five years I was in and out of hospital, collapsing, once to the point almost of death, with very severe attacks.

But during a remission, I was interviewed at London University and was accepted on to their External Diploma in Social Studies. They warned me I was a bit old to be thinking of getting a job when I'd completed the course! I think doing it was one of the very nicest experiences I've ever had. It was a new course, held in Guildford and as guinea pigs we mature students became very supportive of each other. I was with twelve other women, two days a week. We had practical work placements, a wonderful way to understand other people's jobs. I did one placement in an old peoples' home for four weeks. At first I thought how marvellous, because it was purpose-built, and seemed to have rather a hotel atmosphere. But a week later I thought completely differently. I remember seeing an old man (a self-respecting countryman) tremble from head to foot because he'd just come in and had to be bathed. Their pension books were taken away from them, and they had to queue up weekly for their pocket money – they didn't seem to see it as their own money. The 'good' ones were the ones who kept quiet and sat still. And they weren't allowed to bring in any personal possessions bigger than a cushion. I went on to do another placement of great importance to me on the issue of adoption.

Sometimes I had to study in hospital, ill with asthma, and then a hysterectomy. Post-operatively I got severe asthma again and landed in intensive care, but I recovered, and passed. I was ticked off by one nursing sister for having dusty books on my locker.

Almost at the moment I qualified, and was applying for jobs, my husband retired. He was now in ill health and so, for me, a job became out of the question. I'd thought he'd still be up in London three days a week, and that I'd at least be able to get a part-time job. Perhaps I'd been acting with a degree of over-optimism, as underneath I think I'd always felt his health would be a problem. So I did voluntary work at the local Citizens Advice Bureau one and a half days a week for the next two years. Of course, dispensing information is important, but I'd wanted to get much more deeply involved, especially in the area of adoption. I'd have liked to have been making policy, but this was not possible at the CAB, which cannot specialise.

I'd always been a feminist, ever since I can remember. During my course I'd noticed that women were pretty well ignored. Even sociology avoided any mention of the position of women, who were marginally referred to in terms of 'the family'. At this period there was a big build-up of family life. Maternal deprivation theories were at their height! It sounds odd, but there was a book I got out of the library, *Music and Women*, by Sophie Drinker written in 1948, which I renewed 15 times! It's now been reprinted, so I own my own copy. It isn't known in feminist circles today and I can't get anyone to read it, but it's incredible. Sophie Drinker looks at some of the hopeful religions and belief systems of the past. During the first millennium BC these were pretty much destroyed by men. She discusses the way that the idea came about that the flesh is evil and that women are responsible for sin and temptation. She looks at how what had once been the source of women's power and authority now became the very reason for their supposed wickedness and inferiority. Women's rites were taken away from them and they were excluded from religious offices, music and education. She points out how obscene it is to see a procession of little choirboys, with no girls. Obviously this book had a profound influence on me! It coalesced many ideas for me, and I wrote to the London Women's Liberation Workshop, asking them to put me in touch with my local women's group. I remember how moved I was when I got my first letter (their reply) signed 'In Sisterhood'. It was like a door opening into a new world. They introduced me to a Guildford Women's group. Here we decided to do something practical: to try to establish a Women's Aid refuge in the area – there's nothing in

Surrey, even today. After five years of struggle, the council finally managed to destroy us. I've got a pile of fascinating documents about it – a story of its own, should anyone ever want to illustrate how these things are blocked and crushed.

Meanwhile I gave up my voluntary work in the CAB because I'd got on to a post-graduate social research course. I got on to it as a non-graduate on the strength of a piece I'd written about adoption. And this . . . is where I really came unstuck academically! If only I'd known more, I'd have taken a preliminary course in statistics beforehand, but they said on the prospectus you didn't need any prior knowledge of this subject. It was just like doing a Latin 'A' level without ever having done any Latin before. Under better circumstances, I'm sure I could have managed, but meanwhile my husband's illness was very much worse, and this was draining me, too. Other things there also did not help: none of my years of unpaid work and experience counted for anything, and on the form we filled in saying what work you'd done, they made me leave mine blank. The only person on the course similarly blank was a very young man who'd never been to work. Then I wrote an essay on Women's Aid, and my (woman) tutor said she'd have given me a 'first' for it, but for the fact that I had prior knowledge. So what with one thing and another, I left after one year, half way through.

My husband's serious illness steadily worsened and so did the pain. Doctors can tackle terminal pain and acute pain, but they still can't always control constant pain. My husband had a terrible fear of going into hospital, and asked me to promise him that he wouldn't have to go in again. He was petrified, thinking he'd never come out, and he couldn't even bear to go for tests. We visited innumerable specialists to try to find him some relief. Finally they supplied me with disposable plastic syringes and taught me to give him painkilling injections myself . . . which I did, for ten years. I was flattered at first at the trust imposed on me. But later it became the most totally agonising thing I'd ever known. First, I felt the injections were bad for his health generally; second, more and more had to be given to get the same effect; and third, it went on so long, and he had to have so many, that it came to dominate both our lives. He could need one at any time of the day or night for eight years. And finally there were no more sites to give the injections. It was totally horrific – all that with someone you love. I realise other people go through terrible things, but this seemed so utterly awful.

One of the last desperate things was to get under the care of a neurologist, who told us that the combination of drugs he'd been taking were a chemical nightmare, and counter productive. From now on, he took some drugs by mouth, and the doctor would come, when called, to give morphine. There were one or two occasions then when I nearly broke: such as when I saw one doctor standing outside my husband's room and he explained he was 'just listening to hear if he really was in pain'.

My husband wanted to keep his illness a secret from everyone, including the children. This made the situation ten times worse and I was often overcome by a fantastic feeling of loneliness. Later, it turned out that the children had known all along from seeing me with the syringe concealed behind my back so many times! They say they would have preferred to have been taken into my confidence.

He was very courageous, and we did have some fun. He'd wake up about 4.30 a.m., in pain and I'd make some tea, and we'd sit up talking or playing childish guessing games till 10.30. Sometimes just talking took his mind off the pain better than drugs.

This went on throughout my 50s. One evening, after a happy day, he died suddenly of a cerebral haemorrhage. I don't think he suffered, or knew anything about it, so my first feelings were of relief. Then the shock left me numb for many months, but I had the feeling I mustn't sit still and think about it, that I must get on. The most important thing had growingly become 'The Cause' – equality for women, of course, and I don't mean merely equal opportunities! I felt I wanted to become totally and single-mindedly devoted to that. So here I am just about to finish a course in Women's Studies at the Polytechnic of Central London. It's been excellent, offering me structured reading, clearing my mind. It's definitely been the resolution of an ambition, but it's by no means the end.

I still feel a big gap. And I can feel myself changing, to take up again parts of myself I had put aside during my marriage. A great bone of contention between us was religion. Originally, when we met, I was a keen high church Anglican, while he was a positive atheist, and very joyful about it. It took him two years of incessant argument to make me agree with him with my *reason*. If I hadn't given in to him the marriage would have been off. He just couldn't rest until he'd got me thinking the way he did, and this continued throughout our married life. I became a reluctant agnostic. I was never able to agree with him in my *feelings*, and he could never appreciate that my religious feelings were part and parcel of a desire for goodness and a better world. As it was, however much I tried to bury this bone of contention, it just kept on surfacing again. We wouldn't argue about it exactly, but a situation would arise, about once a week there'd be a report in the paper, say, about a church collapsing and killing a whole group of priests in South America, and he'd say, 'Ah, there you are, that's your God for you,' and I'd reply, 'How simplistic!' and he'd say, 'See you haven't changed after all these years.' He'd get angry, and I'd get tearful. The children thought this was a big joke, since it carried on for years! And of course, I'd never cheated, bringing them up to be agnostic, exactly as he wanted. I felt it was a terrible thing to be compelled to give up my views.

Probably the appeal to reason is insufficient to alter feelings. Perhaps if I had read 'Heaven' by Rupert Brooke earlier I would have been able to *laugh* at some of my feelings and that would have saved a lot of argument. This poem by him is about a fish's idea of heaven!

Fish say, they have their Stream and Pond;
But is there anything Beyond?
This life cannot be All, they swear,
For how unpleasant, if it were!
One may not doubt that, somehow, Good
Shall come of Water and of Mud;
And, sure, the reverent eye must see
A Purpose in Liquidity . . .
But somewhere beyond Space and Time,
Is wetter Water, slimier slime!
And there (they trust) there swimmeth One
Who swam ere rivers were begun . . .
And under that Almighty Fin
The littlest fish may enter in.

Reconciling the idea of an omnipotent, all-loving God with the amount of suffering in the world is asking too much. As far as I can see most religious leaders dodge this issue. However, if the Divine is thought of as being within us all and if, as the feminist theologian Mary Daly suggests, we define God not as a noun but as a verb (*to be*, presumably) this dilemma is on the way to being resolved. We could get away, too, from the harmful and impoverishing notion that the deity is of the masculine gender.

I could not take Christianity hook, line and sinker ever again, as I have come to see what a very bad influence it has been on and for women, teaching them to be guilt-ridden and submissive. Researching an essay on 'The Ordination of Women', I found that there have been numerous accounts of the creation. The ones showing Eve as well as Adam being made in the image of God have been suppressed and the emphasis put on Eve as the wicked temptress. (As children we were conned: we weren't supposed to applaud Eve for having a mind of her own.)

It was not the sexist terminology of religion that triggered off my awareness of just how biased our language is. Dictionaries told me many times over that man (male) is courageous, frank, dignified, just and strong, while at best woman is tactful, modest and compassionate, but is just as likely to be weak, timid and frivolous. Even my most up-to-date dictionary (Collins, 1979) describes female characteristics as 'meekness and cowardliness'. But it was *old woman* that really hit me. *Old man* is a term of endearment; *old woman* can be applied to either sex as a term of abuse. When a timid, fussy man is described as 'a proper old woman', how are senior citizens (feminine gender) supposed to feel about the implied slight? To get anywhere near *old man*, *old woman* has to be upgraded socially to *old lady* or rejuvenated to *old girl*. This is an example not only of double standards, but of putting over flagrant untruth. The evidence is that *old women* are better at looking after themselves at 70 plus than their male counterparts. I know *old women* of 80 plus who not only grow their own vegetables but supply their neighbours!

Our ordinary everyday language is a most formidable obstacle to women in their struggle for justice. Apart from anything else, their achievements get lost under the confusing term 'man' (which means humanity but also means male). So what do we understand by 'Man with his mighty brain was a tool-using animal'? So ingrained are these habits of language that when I saw a newspaper heading 'Lonely 65-year-old skier crosses Alps', I mistakenly imagined this was a male feat.

There is no word for female strength to correspond with 'virility': ideas about women's lesser physical strength have been used to impute mental inferiority and are extremely misleading. As well as the obvious things like women living longer, being less susceptible to a wide range of diseases, producing two-thirds of Third World food and from time immemorial being the water-carriers of the world . . . what about their athletic potential? I soon found out (reading Janice Kaplan's *Women and Sports* and Dr K. F. Dyer's *Catching up the Men*) just how underestimated this has been. 'By 1995,' Dr Dyer (a man) calculates, 'women's average performance in all major track events will match that of men and the marathon record will be well within a woman's grasp by 1990.'

We should not take anything for granted. And I think the habit of questioning (which I learnt from my husband) is what really keeps me going: it makes the newspapers, TV, books, radio, people generally . . . of eternal fascination.

At this point I begin to worry about being disloyal: as though I've made the best of men, my husband, seem like a tyrant. I have been challenged on this score from time to time: 'How can you possibly be a feminist when you've got such a marvellous husband?' Well, he was a feminist, too, or so he thought. 'Women only wear high heels', (which he hated), he would say, 'to shorten their stride and make men feel superior.' But the funny thing was that although he wanted women in general, and his daughters in particular, to have careers, he didn't want me to do anything at all *outside* the home. In that way, without realising it, he carried the mantle of the patriarchal oppressor. I can see him smiling wryly at the thought. But it seems to me infinitely sad.

Meanwhile, I still live from day to day (no bad thing, enjoying each day for itself) and often feel lonely especially at weekends and in the evening. Those nice companionable times I had with him have just vanished. Also, like many women of my age, I've lost two very warm, close women friends who died about the same time as my husband. But I'm still involved in women's groups. I am proud to be an early member of the Older Feminist Network. I suppose, more than anything else now, what I'd like to do is to reach women who are unaware of the meaning of the women's movement, or even hostile to it.

CHAPTER 9

A Career in Jazz

Kathy Stobart

I was brought up in South Shields, Durham, the baby of the family with two brothers. I started to play music at 14, and I'd always wanted to entertain. Actually, I started off by singing and dancing, and didn't get serious about becoming a saxophonist until I was 16, when I joined a band as a singer and saxophonist in Newcastle-upon-Tyne.

The bandleader took me on because I was young and easy to manipulate. He was also saving himself an extra fee for a singer. I had an open, fresh mind, and I was keen: it was a fantastic experience. We were doing twelve three-hour sessions a week in the 'Oxford Galleries'. That's how I began to think, breathe and eat music. It was the first time I'd heard jazz records. Being surrounded by all those male musicians, and the right exposure to jazz, really put me in the mould, along with increasing the discipline in my playing. Music is my life. I've been playing the saxophone for 45 years now, and there is still a great deal of playing in me.

My father was a policeman and tyrannical, which was a shame for him as it made him miss out on a lot of love. The only time you could bring a smile to his face was if you did something he could be proud of. Fortunately we all did, mainly in the area of sports. My brothers in their youth were both very athletic, one an excellent runner and the other a champion swimmer. But the effect of me having a father like that was to make me terrified of men, and at the same time probably contributed to my getting married so young, to get away from home. I was 18. That marriage lasted for five and a half years. He was a very nice man, but I was far too young really, and consequently it was a bit of a disaster. He was a Canadian, and wanted us to go and live in California where there were supposed to be many opportunities. At that time there were all-women jazz bands in America, but I was unusual because I was playing in an all male band. This meant my playing ability had to be very high, and in fact I was considered to be one of the top tenor players in the country when I was 18. But America was the 'big sell' and I didn't want that pressure, so in the end I stayed in London and he went back.

My mother, as a wife of a policeman in those days, wasn't allowed to take any paid work. She expressed her immense musical talent through playing the piano at functions, getting music lessons for us in exchange. She gave us a huge amount of musical encouragement. She came from a large Victorian family and all ten children played with the parents and grandparents. She continued to play until she died at 86.

Soon after my second marriage, when I was 26, my parents came south to live in the house next door. When my second husband, Burt, died, my mother, who was widowed by then, helped considerably with bringing up my sons, who were by then teenagers.

During the 1950s and 1960s I supported the family through playing with the Humphrey Lyttleton Band, first as deputy for Tony Coe, and later joining them permanently. My husband, Burt, was a musician too, but was ill for a long time, which meant I was forced to take on extra work in a music shop three days a week. It pained Burt a great deal that I was playing when he could not, but we so badly needed the income that I couldn't give up on that account. It was a difficult period. He died when he was just 40. He was an alcoholic, but he was also addicted to a cough mixture which is a renowned liver killer, so the combination was fatal.

It was a great shock to me to discover he was an alcoholic. The doctor told me one day, assuming I already knew. It was like someone clouting me over the head with a brick, I was that unprepared for it. I discovered his addiction to cough mixture when one day, just to unwind, I went to clear out an old cupboard at the top of the stairs. Dozens of empty bottles fell out: it was just like something out of a film. The problem for Burt was lack of adequate treatment. There just weren't the resources available.

I was pretty resilient though, what with working in the music world from so young, and later having three boys within five years! Coping with all those dirty nappies for four and a half years makes you pretty resilient! My relationship with my sons has been terrific. Although the teenage years are not a good time for a child's father to die, none of them went off the rails, and of course my mother was a great help. My relationship with her was always good, and we definitely had some extra-sensory perception between us. She could be watching the telly, and completely unlinked to what was on, she'd start a sentence in the middle, like, ' . . . he shouldn't have said that,' and I'd know immediately what she meant. We'd get feelings about things as well: if I was looking for something, she'd have a little think, and then bang, she'd home in on where it was, even if it was right at the bottom of a drawer that hadn't been opened for ages. The night she died I'd been worried about her because she'd had a bad cold for a few days. Although I'd bought her an electric overblanket, I knew she wouldn't keep it switched on all night, because she'd worry about the cost and the safety, even though I'd told her I'd got one that was so safe you could practically put it in the washing machine and it would be all right. That night she was sitting in the chair in front of the fire and I was telling her I wanted to call the doctor out, but she wouldn't have it. Later she went to bed and passed away in her sleep. You'd never believe it, but this is the anniversary of the night she died: that's a bit of a coincidence. It's funny how you always think about all the things you didn't do for someone once they die. I wished I spent more time talking with her, instead of flying in and out a lot of the time, and yelling a few words to her about the boys. But of course you can never do anything different, really. We used to think that we looked after her, but really it was the other way around.

On the whole I've had great support too from other musicians over the years. Basically I've been working pretty consistently since I was 17 and I'm now 59. My playing philosophy has always been to play how I feel it. You can only play the jazz that you hear in yourself. I've never tried to emulate anybody, and I'm not distracted by the pursuit of a perfect technique. I can do all the fancy frills when aroused, but I tend to play within a simple form. I've always described myself as playing in the modern/mainstream jazz mould, veering more to the modern.

Whether it's to do with my being a woman, or just pure discomfort because I play well, I've encountered several men who blocked me and cut off important channels of work. For instance, the Jazz Centre is very important to musicians because of its command of bookings, particularly of London gigs. Despite my success, the chap who was head there one year told me there was no available spot for me to fill in a major London jazz festival, even though a friend of mine had seen a request from the BBC for me to play in a televised broadcast from the festival. It made me furious, but there was nothing I could do about it. The Newcastle Jazz Festival was the same – it was always like getting blood out of a stone. There was no sense or justice in it, for after all Betty Smith, Barbara Thompson and I were the foremost lady saxophonists in the world. I had similar struggles with the BBC in the 1950s. Although I could sometimes get a guest spot on other people's shows, I was never able to have a spot in my own right. I wasn't the only woman in this predicament.

It was fairly soon after Burt died in 1969 that I became a permanent member of the Humphrey Lyttleton Band, which enabled me to go on supporting my family, and took me touring all over the world. I played with Humphrey for eight years and during that time I also formed my own band with Harry Beckett. I decided to leave Humphrey and put all my energies into this new band. This was another very difficult period, and although we had fantastic reviews, the Jazz Centre hardly helped us at all, and this was definitely when I needed that help the most. It took a lot of effort, but we pulled through. Although playing with Humphrey had been a very useful and rewarding period, it had repercussions when I left, as my reputation had been moulded by the music I'd been playing with him. This made the transition into the modern/mainstream more difficult.

Meanwhile I took up teaching at the City Literary Institute to subsidise my living expenses. I started with one small class, and this has now grown to three classes, a big band, and an overspill class. There are actually a hundred budding saxophonists, many of them women, passing through these classes every week!

The result of twelve years' teaching has been the straining of my vocal cords in the endeavour to be heard over 20 or more saxophones eagerly blasting out. Recently I've had to have an operation to remove some nodules. It's all meant quite long periods of not being able to work. My voice is getting better, but I have to use a microphone in class in order to be heard, which is a real bind. I've also gone back to the music shop to work four days a week.

I'm still teaching and playing, but I think it will be time quite soon to retire gracefully. I don't want to be seen as 'the old lady who plays the saxophone'. That's not the image I'd feel comfortable with. I've still got plenty of music left in me, but I think I'll stop gigging in a couple of years. I like teaching because of sharing playing the saxophone with others, and the financial security it brings. But the feeling of playing in a really tight saxophone section in a big band is terrific. If you can sit all night and get eight bars of that magic unity with the lead alto player, where it's just as if you're fingering the notes and he's playing it, you'll float out of that place like you've been let into one of the greatest secrets of the world. It's called ecstasy.

The last eighteen months have been very difficult, what with my nodules, and the subsidence of my house which is in the process of being rebuilt. We're living in a permanent state of disarray and dust, which doesn't help my throat, but we've got to come out of it soon! In the long term I'd like to get a pub with Lenny, who is presently living with me. He moved in last September, and it's a bit of a perfect love story really. I've known him for years: he's a musician as well. About three years ago we were thrown together, and a very special kind of love developed which has a lot to do with love between people involved in a common world. We tried to resist it at first by saying, 'Well, forget it,' and, 'We won't phone each other,' and then of course one of us would. I think the longest we went was six days. Anyway, we now have a great dream to get a pub, which would mean I could still be in touch with what's happening in the jazz world, while bowing out gracefully. That's my plan, and as long as my health holds up, I'm optimistic about the future.

CHAPTER 10

Strong Love, Strong Grief

Daphne Mimmack

The decision to write my personal feelings about grief came to me because there seems to be very little written on the subject. Unlike grief everyone is prepared for love in so many ways – hundreds of books and poems, plays and songs have been written on all different kinds of love. Perhaps even if we knew in advance about grief it would still leave us totally unprepared for the way it takes over our minds and bodies. Love motivates, invigorates and stimulates, makes you feel ten feet tall and able to cope with anything. Grief diminishes your stature. Loss of the loved one makes it difficult to carry on with daily living.

My daughter died from suicide when she was 27, after fighting two terrible disabilities. She was both paralysed from the armpits downwards and then subsequently became allergic to almost everything. My uppermost feeling when she died was that she is not in any more pain mentally or physically, and she has no more worry about her long-term care if anything happened to myself or my husband. This I still feel very strongly, but it fades into the background, because the immediate shock of losing someone you love evokes such pain it is impossible to feel anything else.

The first effect of grief was the devastating physical and mental breakdown of my body. In retrospect, several months later, I think nature is so clever. It made it impossible for me to think or feel strongly about other things as I was so concerned about my own needs. Everything required supreme effort. To make a cup of tea left me exhausted. The effort of getting out of bed every day was so exhausting that it was necessary to rest between each little daily task. Every day was a horrible nightmare: the basic chores took so long and required so much of my attention that my body and mind just felt numb.

I experienced the same feelings when my mother died over 30 years ago. I remember going to my local GP because of feeling so exhausted even though I was sleeping well. He prescribed sleeping pills and purple hearts. I only took one of each and learned my first lesson about drugs: it is no use trying to blot out reality. I did not go to a doctor following my daughter's death.

I get great comfort in being near to people who physically cared for Julie, especially her then present and ex boy friends and her most recent girl friend. I felt I could draw on their closeness to Julie. I also got comfort from playing her music tapes. I missed the sounds so much. I liked having her things around to touch them. I also like to wear a sweater of hers: it is all I have left besides memories.

There are so many mixed emotions: anger directed at everything and everyone; contempt – especially towards people who would not acknowledge Julie's death. A great many of those people have hurt me terribly. Ironically they are the same people who hurt Julie when she was alive. I received great comfort from the many people who wrote to me. It was an acknowledgement that Julie once lived. I felt they had taken trouble to sit and think of her. It was much appreciated.

Socialising is still a painful experience. Unless I know the person extremely well, I can only tolerate very short encounters. I made a rule very soon after Julie's death not to allow myself to get into company where there is no escape. After one painful experience I was quite ill when we got home, although the people concerned were very kind and it was no fault of theirs.

There is another side that is difficult to put into words. To me it has no religious connotations. During these long endless months I have great comfort from the feeling that Julie is very close and near. This has receded slightly now but it is a definite and tangible feeling. I believe many people have this experience, and it is a great help in getting through the day.

Outwardly my appearance seems much the same, but inwardly I feel hundreds of years old. I am surprised when I find I can laugh at the same things I used to but it takes longer to reach the core of humour. My mind tends to slip, I can forget things even as I speak of them. In company I find my mind has totally wandered and it requires great effort to come back to earth. Visiting public places where we enjoyed ourselves is especially difficult, and though I do not easily cry, I do so on such occasions.

I do not allow myself to think too deeply about Julie as this again drains me. I cannot want her to live as she did those last months. I grieve not for Julie, but for myself. Grief to me is totally selfish. Love I can spread around, grief I hug to myself.

My husband was and is my greatest support. All the emotions I have expressed he feels in exactly the same way. We can speak of Julie as and when we feel the need without feeling that we embarrass anyone. Some people do not know how to react if Julie is mentioned, which negates her as a person. Dennis and I also look forward to seeing the few personal friends with whom we can speak about Julie freely. Our pets are another source to keep Dennis and me functioning. Our family dog was extremely depressed at the loss of Julie. She also had some terrapins, and even they reacted, refusing food for three months after her death.

I think I am coming to terms with the hardest part of grief. Because life is relentless and doesn't wait for anyone, I am having to re-shape my future. It is unbearable that I am now planning, buying and doing things about which Julie has no knowledge. Death is so final.

CHAPTER 11

A Changing Vision of England

Neela Roy

If I compare my childhood to the average Asian family living in the Indian sub-continent, I feel I was very lucky. My father was a reasonably successful businessman, who really worshipped my mother. He felt that if any man really loved his wife, he wouldn't burden her with many children. He really saw how large families put women under pressure, so although they could have afforded more children I was one of only two. First my brother was born, and later when I arrived, far from thinking I was a burden as a girl, they were delighted. In fact, my father always said I brought him luck, particularly in his business which picked up just after I was born. He used to tell my mother I was his Laxmi – the goddess of prosperity. I always had the sense that I was valuable to him.

My parents lived in Bangladesh, but because they thought the education was better in India, they sent me during term-time to live in Calcutta, where I was looked after by a woman who was like an older sister to me. My Dad used to ring me every Sunday by trunk call. All through my childhood I was very close to him.

But there was great family tension over my brother. My father wanted him so much either to be academic – and become something like a doctor – or to take after him and be good at business. But he isn't at all academic. He is very gifted musically, in playing the sitar, and has a wonderful voice. He never wanted to study academic subjects, and this caused a disastrous situation at home. My mother, who wanted to protect him from my father's pressure, still suffers today from everything she went through with them and the tension between them. She, too, plays the sitar very well, and though she didn't encourage my brother, he must have picked up her interest and talent. My father became so bitter about him, he virtually cut himself off from him, as he just couldn't deal with his attitude. We all suffered greatly from the rift this caused.

My father was in all other respects a very affectionate and generous man, marvellous to me, respectful to my mother, consulting her in all his decisions, and always helping out family and friends, especially where their children's education was concerned. Education – especially of the 'English' kind – was very important to him, such were the attitudes implanted into him. When he fell very ill in 1979, I was by now in England, and married. My mother wanted him to go to hospital in Calcutta, where the medical treatment was better than in Bangladesh, but he refused as he did not want to see my brother, who now lived there. However, eventually he was so ill, so weak, that he had no choice. They went by car to the border, where they were met by my brother. Apparently the moment my brother touched him my father had a stroke, closed his eyes, and didn't open them for another three weeks. My brother stayed by his side the whole time. By the time we arrived from England a few days later he was occasionally opening his eyes, and so he recognised me before he died. I'd wanted to stay with him until the end, but my husband was very anxious about Tinku, our daughter, who was then nearly 3. She had diarrhoea and a heat rash, and he is always very over-anxious about such things, and wanted us to return to England with her. I feel very bitter that he made us return, as my father died the next day.

By that time I'd been married, and living in England, for twelve years. My father had never really wanted me to get married, and said his luck changed for the worse when I did. However, when I was about 21, I began to consider a young man, Dilip, who was quite well known to my family and liked by them. My father respected his academic qualifications. Dilip already lived in England, where he had a work permit. But he was finding life very difficult over here, suffering greatly from loneliness, and from racism. He always remembers his first encounter with racism – a young woman in an employment bureau saying to him, 'It's not *me* but we can't provide coloured people with jobs.' He often says how clearly he can still see that girl's face in his mind, as if it was burnt in. He ended up in hospital eventually with internal bleeding from an ulcer. There was not one Black doctor or nurse, and he felt very isolated. He remembers that two of the cleaners, West Indians, befriended him, taking home his pyjamas to wash and so on, supporting him through 'the feeling of the skin'. Even today when I go to that hospital, St Bartholomew's, I notice it is *still* very white.

All this led to him thinking about me, whom he knew a little, and my family. After a period of correspondence, he came back and married me. I was 22, and studying law at the time. I gave up my studies, because I knew I was going to England, and I had such dreams! I saw England through visions I'd acquired through reading poets like Wordsworth and Keats . . . such brainwashing! Also in my mind what really mattered now was Dilip's education. I would work and look after him, and he would study full-time. I was very excited, and at that time I wasn't all that upset about leaving my family.

My arrival in England, my first visit to Trafalgar Square, the first weeks . . . all very exciting. But soon the struggle, the disappointments began creeping in, and it was then I began to miss them. I was so unprepared in so many ways. My idea of marriage, of love, was very platonic – and remains so. It's not that I was ignorant about sex – I knew all about it. However, it doesn't interest me very much – I feel through *all* the senses, and sex itself isn't necessarily connected with them. There's a difference between myself and Dilip on this. Also, at first, I couldn't cook – didn't know exactly how to use the spices – my father hadn't ever wanted me to learn, or to be taken up with household tasks. It makes me laugh now when all my friends at work think I'm such a marvellous cook.

We came over in the winter, and throughout the spring and early summer, I'd sit in that little bedsitter in Finsbury Park staring out of the window all day, so bored. Dilip treated me like his baby – don't go out alone, don't cross the road on your own, this will happen, that will happen. 'You don't know this country.' He didn't think I'd be able to get a job – nor did my brother, who'd kept laughing at my English in Calcutta, telling me I'd never cope here. But one day that summer we went up to the West End with a Bengali woman friend, who showed us an employment bureau she'd got a job from. She was supporting her husband who was also studying. Through this bureau I got an interview with the Eagle Star Insurance Company. Dilip was so nervous, wondering how I was going to cope. I filled out a form there, and while I was doing so, I could hear my interviewer over the partition ringing the bureau and saying very angrily that 'she's come in her dress' – referring to my sari. I couldn't understand why this mattered. I could see why someone would be annoyed with me if I behaved badly, but racist attitudes – skin – I just could not understand. By the time I'd finished the form, he was back, being very polite and nice to me, telling me I was to go to the Monument branch, to become a figure clerk. Then, so typical of English people, he said, 'I admire your sari, but just one thing, you'll have to work in a skirt in the office.' Of course, I had to agree, and at that time I didn't see entirely what a big issue this was. He explained how to get to the Monument, and off I went – the first time ever I'd travelled around London on my own. I went into a closed lift on my own – feeling terrified as it wasn't like lifts at home – and kept smiling all the way, thinking, 'This feels good; Dilip will be proud of me.'

I'd told them I could start in two weeks, and they sent me a letter to confirm it. But Dilip was angry about the fact I was not allowed to wear a sari, and told me to write back saying I'd work there for a month to earn the money to buy dresses, and wear my sari for that time. By return came a letter saying the job had now gone – so I had two, one accepting me, and one contradicting it.

After this I couldn't get a job for a long time, though I tried with many applications. I became more and more depressed, and finally got conditionally accepted by the Civil Service Commission, who had to check my papers with Calcutta. Because there was at that time some internal trouble in the university, clearance was seriously delayed, and I remained unemployed.

Feeling very depressed and mentally low, with people saying to me, 'Why don't you take just any job?' I went to work for a while in a launderette. It was terrible. The male customers treated us so cheaply, always touching us. The thought of it! I couldn't see how the others could bear it. And I thought of my Dad and my family – what on earth would they think of me doing this? I soon became very ill with asthma attacks, and had to go into hospital. I felt very close to Dilip then, suffering what he had been through. I worried a lot about how he'd manage.

Eventually, my clearance came through and I got the Civil Service job, as a clerical assistant. I worked there for ten years, until I was 32. Of course, I had higher qualifications than this grade needed, but it was not until five years into the job that the supervisor looked through my papers, saw this, and promoted me overnight to clerical officer. I made a good friend there: an elderly and very 'English' man, nearing retirement, and his wife. He used to invite me and Dilip to his house, but however nice they were, there was always some tension – his wife would get in a state over what to cook.

Gradually I was making more friends among Indians, most of whom I met through Dilip. He was becoming involved in the Liberal Party meanwhile, which in my view is another kind of Conservative Party, and we would be invited to various social occasions. Of course, being the only Black woman, I'd be a kind of novelty for them at these parties, with all the usual comments about my sari, and I never felt happy and free with them. Sometimes, meeting them in other settings, like shops, they'd look right through me, pretending they didn't recognise me and that I wasn't there. But I have made some genuine and affectionate English friends. Some of my Indian friends are very close – one is now like an older sister to me.

I didn't really want to have children at all, but when I was about 32, I began to reflect on it more seriously. My closest woman friend, also Asian, told me she thought I was being selfish and ought to be thinking about having a family. My mother also wanted it – my father put no pressure on me. Dilip was qualified by now, we had a house, and he had a job with the *Daily Express*. I noticed that when I was at Indian gatherings, like the Puja festival, I'd look at all the women with their children and think perhaps I was lacking something, and began to feel more emotionally open to having children. But Dilip and I were so irritable with each other all the time, with the added strain of having to make the relationship look all right to friends. However, I decided to try to conceive.

This proved difficult, and I lost babies twice at very early stages. Dilip accused me of not really wanting them. Then I got pregnant again, and lost the baby at three months, landing up in hospital. Dilip was very protective during the pregnancy – 'You go and lie down.' Once I really broke down, and cried. He asked, 'Why? Why? What's wrong?' and I couldn't ever say. Now, I can never cry any more in front of him because he looks and feels so lost when I do, and can't bear any tears from me.

After the miscarriage, we went to Calcutta to visit the family. I'm praying one day I'll be able to go on my own. I particularly want to visit my grandmother, who was such a strong woman, managing with a large family in poverty, yet always generous to everybody.

Finally, though she arrived five weeks early, I had my first child, and two years later, my second . . . a mistake that time. I felt so guilty, I wasn't even coping properly with my first, and still felt quite ill. But as Tinku, my daughter, and Rinku, my son, grew older, I began to get involved with other mothers through a playgroup, and began to mix with local women in a different way. I took the playgroup course – very unchallenging, but I wanted to do something – and I made some new friends. It gave me a chance, anyway, to talk about some of my ideas, and about my own culture. I met a woman who was a lecturer in further education, and she asked me to go and give a few talks to her students about her way of life.

I then applied for a job as a crèche organiser with ESL (English as a Second Language) at an adult education centre. I wasn't successful, but they asked me instead to teach ESL there. I would have done, but meanwhile I'd applied for another job, to work in a collectively run Children's Centre, and this time I got the job. This is where I still work today. We are four white and four Black women, and the idea behind the centre is to provide not only childcare, such as playgroup and after-school care for children, but also facilities and activities for women.

At first I carried out outreach work among Asian women in the local community, trying to involve them in the centre, talking with them for many hours. Many of them come from very impoverished communities, and do not speak English at all well. They worry that they will make fools of themselves if they come out more into the community here. It's been hard going with *all* the local women – overcoming their attitude that they just want to use the childcare facilities, and not wanting for various reasons to participate in the courses and activities we run on a drop-in basis. We're now trying to get a steady and regular playgroup established, which we think will help confidence grow. I'm also working on a project involving young Asian women writing about their lives, which we've got a small grant for. This is also uphill work: the pressure is still on us to pretend everything is just fine and not reveal our true feelings. However, it's under way, and I'm hoping it will be published and be successful.

For myself, I'm very happy in this job. We mainly all get along really well. I feel freer there than I have for many years. I love the lack of formality, and being able to say what I really feel, without covering up all the time. I like working with women, and it feels very warm there. Women understand the pressures of life, going from work to the kitchen. We share our experiences, talking openly. I don't have to pretend there that my marriage is all right, and I can take my problems there. I like working with the children, and I really enjoy the administrative side, which I want to do more of. It absorbs me there, mentally and emotionally.

CHAPTER 12

A Singular Strength – From Childhood to Now

Rosina Sligo

When I look at myself now, I can see how certain parts of my character, especially my strong-willed independence, have their beginnings in my childhood. I can see how what happened to me then gave me both strength and a permanent sense of loss, and how, living as I do now completely independent of any family, I grew up feeling that family life was something I've never been a part of, in the way that most people experience it.

Through the force of circumstances of the 1914-18 war, my parents' marriage broke up before I was born. It was very difficult, then, for a woman to keep a child on her own, virtually impossible. So my mother left me with her grandmother, who'd already brought up a great family of her own. I don't know, quite frankly, what happened to my mother. She probably lived with us for a time, and then went off into service to try to earn a living, leaving me with my great-grandmother. She, too, was very poor, working as a machinist from home, making up bolster cases for the local bedding factory. The whole atmosphere was of the Victorian era, which still clung around the first part of the twentieth century, in its furniture, customs and ideas. Since she was always busy, and since there was this huge age gap, I spent many solitary hours in what was (despite being near Paddington Station) a quiet and village-like atmosphere. I can't remember any other children around at all.

Whenever my great-grandmother was ill, or, as once happened, had an accident, I felt terrified, sensing, even at 4 and 5, that she was my only link with life. We saw something of her other children (my great-aunts and uncles) and their families. Meanwhile, though I did not realise who he was at the time, my father was living with one of her daughters. I felt he had an affection for me, but he never acknowledged our relationship.

There was money around in the family – part of it owned the factory she worked for. But my great-grandmother saw very little of it, and that more like a charity handout. She was just as exploited as all the other workers in that paternalistic way, with a Christmas box of food every year from a farm in Kent. They got joints of meat in accordance with their seniority and position in the firm. Eventually one of her property-owning son-in-laws installed us in a flat in Ladbroke Grove.

It was very quiet, there, too, in those days. I remember waking up early some mornings and going out to sit on the steps. Being there in that peace, and feeling totally alone, is what I now think of as having been a kind of mystical experience. When I was nearly 7, I remember things getting busier around the time of the General Strike, with lorries rushing up and down the road. I know that my father was a special constable against the strikers, with a striped armband and truncheon.

Although we were poor, I had clean dresses, and my great-grandmother curled my hair. I must have looked very pretty. Unless she'd worked hard, how could she have supported us? The state pension in those days was very small. I didn't notice my difference from other children, say at Christmas and birthdays, because I didn't have enough contact with their home lives to be comparative.

It was all part of a building up of that inner strength which I feel I've acquired. I was extremely self-willed, taking myself off on long walks across west London, without telling anyone. I discovered at a very early age that discussion can be a complete waste of time – if you wanted to do something, you just did it, or they'd usually try to stop you.

As was common practice in those days, I used to sleep with my great-grandmother. When I was about 7 or 8, I woke up because she was feeling ill, and drifted off again in the warmth and snugness. In the morning, one of her young granddaughters, who was about 16, and used to come every day to help out, came in and tried to wake her. Realising that she'd died in the night with me beside her, she snatched me up, and rushed with me to the upstairs flat. There I was held by someone, as I burst into tears, realising she was dead, and feeling lost and frightened. I can still feel now that terrible sense of loss.

Soon after, I remember my great-aunt (the one living with my father) asking me where I thought I was going to live now. 'Can't I come and live with you?' I asked. 'No,' she replied, 'I've got too many children of my own.' Of course, I was devastated. It was several years later that I realised what she told me wasn't true, because they went on to have three more children. This was how I came to feel that they just hadn't wanted me, and this sense of rejection went very deep.

Eventually I was taken to live at one of my great-uncles, who had an enormous family. I felt quite overwhelmed by all those people. I found it very difficult in an environment with so many children. I was different, and I was treated differently. My great-aunt told me she couldn't understand me, because I was so unlike her children. She did her very best for me, and was also a very hard-working woman. But now I was more lost and lonely than ever I had been when I was with my great-grandmother. But although I felt like an outcast, I still had my inner thoughts, living in my own world, and often going off into dreams.

I lived there until I was 21, but retaining my separateness. By 16 I was already quite politically aware, going off to street corner meetings, and reading left-wing books by authors like Upton Sinclair and Bernard Shaw. I began to take a great interest in Communist ideas and speakers.

This is the pattern laid down in my childhood and youth which formed the basis of the woman I grew to be. Now I am older, I can see the same strengths and self-will coming through, as these incidents from my later years show.

One thing that has happened to me of considerable consequence in my later life is the matter of my hip. It's really imprinted on my brain how it all happened. I was walking back from the village at dusk and I can remember it exactly. I suddenly experienced a strong ache in my hip. I'd been having slight pains for some time, but this was different. It really disturbed me, and set off in me a sense of foreboding. I remember getting home to my cottage and sitting down feeling anxious, and when I came to stand up, the pain made me feel that something rather terrible was happening to me. It was a worrying and wearying time anyway, because I was trying to sell my cottage and find a flat to move to in London without any one to support me.

The next morning I felt just as worried about my hip, so I got in my van (which I had then for my business) and drove off to the surgery to make an afternoon appointment to see the doctor – then off to the estate agent to see how things were proceeding with the sale of my cottage. I told her, close to tears, that something was very wrong with me. Then, reluctant to go home and be there in pain on my own till my four o'clock appointment, I went to sit outside the church. When I came to get back into the van I felt terribly distressed, because I couldn't lift my leg up, and had to pick it up with both hands and put it into the van. I did go home, where I had a bad nose bleed, only to return to the doctor's to be told he couldn't examine me properly in this state. He took my blood pressure, and told me to return next week.

The next day I tried to walk using a stick, but it was so painful and difficult, I had to turn back in tears of pain and fear. Over the next few days the pain became indescribable and unbearable. Nothing afterwards could touch it. Then there followed various visits to the doctor's (one told me I had arthritis), and quite frankly I was simply left on my own to cope, the general attitude being that I should pull myself together.

Eventually my temperature was so high, I got carted off to the local hospital, where I was thought to have a gynaecological problem. Then they diagnosed an abcess on my appendix. I was in there for a total of two weeks, and the pain did not lessen. I was made to walk, using a frame. They even sent me to see a psychiatrist. Christmas approaching, they discharged me, saying I had no symptoms and no temperature.

One of my friends could see this wasn't so. Shocked at the state I was in, she drove me to London, where I was again admitted to hospital. Again, I was put through various painful gynaecological examinations, including a D and C operation in which they had to give me a blood transfusion. Then they put me on a scanner, and finally diagnosed me as having a hip problem! They did not have enough of my blood group to operate, so meanwhile I was put on traction, and at last I was made more comfortable.

All this time, of course, I'd felt my hip crumbling away. Why didn't I complain more when I was made to put my weight on it and walk? I'd got locked into my own silence, internalising, not saying things. Finally I had my operation for the removal of the head and neck of the femur which were very badly infected. I was on my back for six weeks, with massive doses of antibiotics and painkilling tablets, injections against blood clots and heavily nursed. Suddenly it came to me: one of my legs would be shorter than the other – and at this same time, one of the student nurses asked me if I realised.

Finally I progressed to a wheelchair and to crutches, being taught to move around by physiotherapists. Up until that time I kept cheerful, and had a terrific amount of support from people. I had a wonderful birthday party there. But once I started to grasp the full significance, I began to crack up. While visitors were there I was the great entertainer, showing them all the things I could do, taking it all in my stride. But afterwards, when they were gone, a lot of tears were shed. I took myself off for rides in my chair, isolating myself so people wouldn't see me cry. But I also had some good old trips around the hospital, exploring and visiting other people in there.

All this just when I was looking forward to setting up my bookselling business in London! I felt shattered. This was the final insult, to be incapacitated now, of all times. And then all the apprehension, afraid I'd fall down in the street: would I be able to manage in London at all?

Finally I managed to complete my move. Amazingly, although my friends helped, they just left me in my new flat, completely surrounded by piles of furniture and unpacked boxes, and off they went! And me still on crutches. But I took it all in my stride. It seemed like my whole life was one long struggle to survive.

It took me some while to get to grips with it all. You can't imagine the chaos. Once I was settled, and overcoming some of the physical difficulties, I went to the local doctor as I was beginning to feel I wanted to get to the bottom of how I could so suddenly have come down with this disease. Soon after, a health visitor asked me if I didn't feel very bitter. 'If they'd put you on traction and antibiotics straight away,' she said, 'you would have been cured.' I was taken aback, and very angry. For up until this time, although I knew I'd been badly treated in hospital with a lot of unnecessary pain, and I also knew they'd not at first treated me for the right thing, I never knew until this point that if I'd been properly diagnosed, I needn't have had a permanent disability. As the impact of her statements sunk in, I thought, 'I must get legal advice.'

After a visit to a solicitor I was awarded legal aid, but it was a year or more before I was able to get the necessary expert medical opinion. This was full of inaccuracies, and came across as a thorough-going whitewash. Even the solicitors found it unacceptable. It took another year to get a second report – but he just corroborated with the previous 'expert'. Apparently it all hinges on the difference between 'negligence' and 'error of judgment'. While both reports accept that the initial diagnoses were wrong – errors of judgment – they say no negligence is involved, and therefore no blame can be attached, nor is anyone responsible for the disability which resulted. At this point the solicitors, in their polite way, virtually told me to get lost. In my discussions of the matter with another solicitor, I was told that the insurance companies who would have to pay out in such cases are willing to spend unlimited amounts to prevent compensation – far more than individual amounts of compensation – in order to protect their long-term interests. So I came quickly to realise it's not just the closed shop of the medical profession all protecting each other that you have to fight, but the legal system, out to make their living, and the insurance profession.

Becoming aware of the cynical attitude prevailing in these matters, I realised I had a choice: to go battling on against the odds with them, feeling aggrieved for the rest of my life, or putting it aside – not giving in, but refusing to let them get me down. In no way was I going to let that happen to me. So I dropped it.

All this time I'd been making efforts to improve the ways I could get about. I was afraid of slipping over, especially in the wet. It was difficult to get onto buses, and at first I couldn't manage the tube. Bit by bit my willpower overcame my fear, because my character is such that I hate to show signs of weakness. My image of myself is that the world can fall down around my ears but I'm not going to let it affect me. I was determined to carry on, and I thought up various schemes to enable me to do so.

I'd always had a car or van before, but my illness and being in hospital had meant selling my last one. Now more than ever I really needed one. At first of course I didn't have the strength or ability to drive, and I could not have managed the worry and expense. But in order to be free, get on with my schemes, and not have to be dependent on others for lifts, I eventually, with the help of long-term friends, managed to buy one, which is beginning to make quite a difference.

As you know, I've always been a very solitary person. Even my nine years in the army was spent with few close relationships. Once when I made some, I was posted far away from them. So I've managed all my life very much on my own. I have had some very good friends. I can mix easily on a superficial level, striking up conversations in a railway carriage, or even in the street, but to enter into a deeper relationship I don't find at all easy. It's only when I have known people for a number of years that I realise a relationship has grown up. Some of my very closest friends have now died, and the ones who are still alive I find I've known for 20 or 40 years.

When I look back, I can see my very best friendships have been with those where the set-up is that you don't have to be involved the whole time. You have to have independent interests on each side. That's when I've felt close, but relatively at ease. Whenever I've had a romantic notion about someone, it hasn't on the whole worked out. Possibly the reason for that is my high expectations which are too much for people to cope with, and probably even for myself as well.

On the other hand, for all the advantages of living alone, I am thinking of a way I might live with others. I was driving along a country road one day about ten years ago when I suddenly realised that the best thing for me would be to live in a community. By this I don't mean communal living, which is a totally different set-up, although I can see there is something in it, and for some people it is an economic necessity. I was making plans to explore this matter further and had made an initial visit to a community, when this hip disaster befell me, setting me back. However, people live there in a common purpose, usually based on some underlying religious or philosophical belief. I'm not sure I've a sufficiently developed spirituality to make a commitment to any one religion or philosophy. In any case, I feel they all have common factors, particularly peace and love. But at first at least I would like to live in one as a lay person, making a contribution along with others towards these common aims, and intend now to continue to explore the possibility in respect of a particular Buddhist community. I just hope my character, which is to say the least a bit on the sharp side, will cope with it, and that I'll be able to submerge my ego to the extent that I wouldn't always feel that my ideas were necessarily right and paramount!

CHAPTER 13

Growing out of Convention

Margaret Strong

I was a very conventional wife, and initially what I wanted was a conventional marriage. I thought I wanted children, but as time went on and children didn't come, I began to examine my reasons for wanting them. I realised that it was only because I was curious to know how they would turn out. My husband was never really very interested in children, and I could see that if I had any, I'd be left to cope, and he would have carried on with his activities. The turning point for my attitude came on my return to full-time work after six years of part-time. This brought with it great job satisfaction. But for many years more I remained in all other respects a perfectly conventional wife, doing all the cooking and cleaning, which I continued to do right up until the end of the marriage. I don't know why, or what I was trying to prove to the world. I saw it as my duty, yes, but also as my domain, and I didn't particularly want him helping with it.

With the return to full-time work came greater freedom. I was spending more time out of the home environment, I had status, and I was a person in my own right. About a year before I went back to work full-time, my husband went on a course at Cambridge, and this is where he met the woman he began a long-term involvement with. The patterns established at that time became quite important to my later thinking, because he thought it was perfectly all right to be away all week, every week, coming home at weekends with everything laid on, whereas when I did a part-time higher degree some years later, he gave me no support whatsoever.

As the years passed, the element of companionship in the marriage grew less and less. I looked for it continually, but it wasn't there. He found it more important to do his manly things. Football, at which he was an excellent amateur, always came first. It provided him with the excuse to go off for weekends, and eventually, since I was obviously not going to be able to change this passionate interest, I began to enjoy these brief spells to do what I wanted and see people I wanted to see. One of our problems was that he'd always put difficulties in the way of us seeing my friends and relatives. He only liked to see his friends, mainly made at work or through football, who were always couples. I had more or less nothing in common with them, except for one or two of the wives. One of these still remains one of my closest friends. I remember those occasions as ones where David and the other husbands competed to take over the conversations, while the wives, with the exception of my friend, would keep themselves very much in the background.

Early on I would myself have liked to have played more sport, but he wouldn't take any interest in that. Nor would he attend any of my social events at work – while of course assuming that I'd attend all of his. I went on playing it this way for many years. Much later on, a mutual friend reported back to me that he now recognises how little enthusiasm and support he'd given to any of my interests.

What we had in common was the home we'd built up together, and also some very good holidays, where we enjoyed the same things. We'd have a pleasurable trip abroad, and then sink back into the gradually growing gulf between us. Unfortunately, he developed a hip problem, which made him less active, but then music replaced his passion for sport – and I'm not musical at all. Then, consciously or unconsciously, he'd let all his marking pile up, so that whenever we had any relatively free time, he'd use it as an excuse to go off and work.

Gradually all the time we'd have to share things trickled away. The sexual side of it died, and with it, much of the affection. I think he may have been having a sporadic affair all this while with the woman he'd met in Cambridge. As alienation set in, and with him spending more weekends at home because of his lessening participation in sport, I began to find myself thinking, 'Oh my God, I can't face this when I retire and have it every day!'

I'd begun to look in my work, and especially with my students, for the affection and companionship missing at home. I became quite involved with some of my groups getting to know them as individuals, as their personal tutor, and socialising with them. They'd sometimes come and visit me at home when he was away – because he'd make it feel so awkward when he was there. They were often the only women I knew who weren't married, or involved in a 'closed' couple with a man, and I found relating to them much easier and refreshing. If they had boy friends, they certainly didn't think of them as the be-all and end-all of their lives. We were often a close group, and our discussions were free and rewarding. Eventually these experiences predisposed me to be able to develop a relationship of great closeness with one of them.

As a tutor I was aware of the dangers of becoming too closely involved with students. Despite our good discussions, I usually kept a formal distance, waiting until after they'd left college if I wanted to have a closer friendship. Inevitably, over the years there were some with whom I would develop a lasting mutual respect and affection. Then something happened which changed my attitude about holding back too much. One student with whom I had a particularly close friendship was killed in a car crash soon after leaving college while on Voluntary Service Overseas. I was devastated – and amazed at the support I received, at how many people had realised how much she'd meant to me.

She and her companions were the first students I'd risked getting a bit close to before they left – and after she'd died I realised I was glad I had taken that risk, otherwise I would have missed knowing her well. Nevertheless, it was some years later until I met another student who wanted from me the same kind of support and affection – and this time I did not hesitate to respond. It was about eight years ago, when I was 44. I was immediately drawn to her, remembering her distinctly from the interview. Within a few weeks of starting the course, she found herself in a lot of difficulties, needing support which I readily gave. Within a few months we became very close. Her turmoil, caused by personal and family problems, went on all that year, and she needed continual help.

During her second year, we began to spend social time together, and a reluctance to part at the end of our evenings began to make itself felt. We very much wanted to spend time in each other's company. At first I really didn't see the way things were going, even though when she came to stay with me my husband was away. We became physically as well as emotionally close. By now my husband had become extremely cool and withdrawn, while she was all warmth and affection. Eventually we slept together. Neither of us had thought of ourselves as lesbians, despite the overtones of sexuality creeping into it. The first time we slept together we felt we were doing it just to be close – not to have to part for the night. It was for both of us a totally new experience.

I can remember there was this imminent parting – both off on our respective holidays for six weeks. Would we sustain what we felt? I went off to a meeting at college thinking, 'Is this really me?' I felt almost disembodied: strange, but good. From there on it all went quite rapidly – I thought about her a great deal. It was intense, and we spent as much time together as we could, without making it obvious. But I made it clear to my husband that I was seeing her, and I think he guessed we were sleeping together.

In my mind I blamed him as much as myself for the final breakdown of our marriage. Communication between us was finished. It came to a head one Saturday when he said I was avoiding every opportunity to be with him! I told him then that I wanted to leave him. He was shattered – just didn't believe it. The only thing he could keep saying was, 'What about all these things we've built up together?' meaning the material things, like the house and possessions. Then he suggested that he wouldn't go away quite so often, and would try to make amends, but it was too late. I don't really understand why he wanted to hang on. I thought he'd welcome his freedom, especially in view of his affair. But in the end it was him being the one rejected, and I suppose that's what hurt – he didn't expect it to finish that way.

Essentially in my mind then grew the need for freedom in all repsects – to come and go as I pleased, to allocate the use of my time as I wanted and where I wanted, spending time with someone if I loved them. I wanted to reject the institution of marriage which I saw as restricting my freedom and development.

The difficulty was that in order for me to find anywhere to live on my own, we would have to sell our jointly owned house, and he would only agree if he got a larger proportion, on the grounds that I earned more and could afford a better mortgage – and that it was me who wanted to go. This was unfair, because I'd never had a separate account, always pooling everything, and of course over the years he'd contributed much less, and I'd to some considerable extent supported him.

After a drawn-out tussle, a settlement was reached, enabling me to get a mortgage on a small flat in London, where I felt I could be more in the centre of things. I became interested in the women's movement, deliberately going out to meet more feminists. By the time I was settling into London, my relationship with my lover was beginning to diminish, mainly because she was becoming involved with someone else. Naturally there were times when I began to wonder if perhaps I'd burnt my boats, though I never once doubted my lesbianism or my feminism. I could never have gone back into living a lie. That would have been more stressful than to battle for survival on my own.

After a couple more years in London, I found I couldn't really settle there. The physical environment was too claustrophobic for me, despite all the facilities and the availability of such things as women's studies on evening courses, which I enjoyed. I decided to move out of the city as I need a certain amount of quietness and solitude which is very hard to achieve when there is a bustle all around you that you are not part of. In the end I decided I would take the risk and move away even though it would be making it harder to maintain the ties with many women I'd made common links with. I found a house in the country that just suited me, and now I continue to travel to London for my work, and for some women's events and groups.

In spite of everything, this move has worked, achieving the object of making me more relaxed. I really enjoy having a garden, and the relative peacefulness of it all, while still having the convenience of local transport, which I can use if I want to get to London. I have a car, too, which is really important, and a telephone.

I can distinguish between solitude and loneliness – an important matter for those who live on their own. Solitude is being able to relax and think things through without continual distraction. Sometimes I experience loneliness, and I define this as feeling 'alone', when you badly want to share thoughts and times with someone else, and there's nobody there. I feel it most on so-called special occasions which just aren't special if there's no one special in your life. Society presses on us that we are meant to celebrate these times and most people want to share them with people they love – birthdays, bank holidays. And the annual holiday thing – people always ask you what you're doing for your holiday, and you think, 'Oh here it comes again.' You end up going through your mind trying to think of someone in a similar situation who might not be 'committed' with whom you have a suitable relationship to spend a couple of weeks. Since most people have families or partners, it is very hard. But there is absolutely no point staying in a relationship where that feeling of common interest has gone, just through fear of this loneliness. If the feeling isn't there, that person is not the one, and it's far better to choose the way on your own, despite all the difficulties.

When I was considering all these matters, about ending my marriage, I found it essential to have the support and advice of other women, particularly those who'd been through the same thing. When I was finally making the break, I was in a women's group, where I was able to talk through all my doubts. I think this is most important for women thinking of leaving their husbands.

Something else that has helped me through all the periods of readjustment is a deep-rooted faith that there must be some reason for life! I was brought up a Catholic and was largely educated at Catholic boarding schools. I spent my holidays with my mother and her family who were not Catholics. So from an early age I was aware of conflicting religious viewpoints and bigotry. I found it difficult to accept some of the narrower Catholic teachings, especially those relating to mixed marriages and the validity of other faiths. However, there is no doubt that for many years my moral judgments and my behaviour were defined by this Catholic influence. You are taught not to question but to accept, and this indoctrination is very effective. It takes time to free yourself of this. I've never been a particularly devout person, or one who has adhered rigidly to religious obligations – I suppose I took the first step away from it all in marrying a man who professed to be a non-believer. Subsequently over the years I've re-examined the teaching of the Church in the light of my feminism and what is happening on a global scale. The result is that I have rejected most of what it stands for, but this has been a gradual and still continuing process. I still retain a belief in what I can only describe as 'life having a purpose': what that purpose is I don't know, and I suppose, given time, I shall continue to search for the answer.

I'm not a political animal. Although I'm a feminist in the sense that I nurture my strength, and share it, by being in discussion groups with other women, I'm not a great campaigner. I admire and respect women who are. I sometimes feel that campaigns won't achieve anything, and perhaps it's because I'm not sufficiently convinced that I don't myself get involved. Am I looking at campaigning in a very limited way? I fluctuate between thinking that the women's action at Greenham Common doesn't change people where it's really needed, and thinking that if everyone was like me, just sitting back, nothing would ever get changed. I remain in a state of ambivalence about this.

Work has remained extremely important to me. Nowadays, though, I don't any longer look for close and affectionate involvement with my students, and I've returned to caring but formal relationships with them. Perhaps I'm getting old! I could make the excuse that I don't have the time, but that's not the case – I always used to find the time. Probably I feel that it is, after all, too dangerous as an emotional risk, or maybe I just don't want it, though I do worry about the potential disappearance of an important source of that kind of affection from my life. Indeed I'm beginning to see that the way my work has more recently developed, it might have been difficult for me to take on any kind of central emotional relationship.

What I really appreciate is how satisyfing and satisfactory it can be to give my work just as much time as I want. When I was married the difficulty was always trying to work out priorities – feeling I shouldn't work in the holidays when I often really wanted to. Now I don't have to feel accountable for how I spend my working time, and I really enjoy that. I can stay on as long as I want without thinking, 'Oh goodness, better not be late home tonight!' Of course men have always had the possibility of staying late at the office! I see in many of my women colleagues those feelings of anxiety and guilt I used to have – worrying away that they may be risking their marriages if they at any time prioritise their jobs or their careers. This is a very common situation in my profession.

Nowadays I have responsibility for running an advanced course in higher education and this continues to demand commitment outside routine working hours. If I were still married it would be very difficult, probably impossible, to handle all those demands. It's also very draining. But I feel very fulfilled. I have no regrets about leaving marriage behind. I feel I'm doing a very worthwhile job, and it gives me a real sense of achievement. Despite the loneliness which sometimes intrudes into my life, I feel I'm in a very productive stage, and I have good friends who give me strength that I need to counter sexist approaches and attitudes which, like all women, I see affecting my everyday life at work – especially in all those undermining, under the surface ways.

CHAPTER 14

Finding the Strong Inner Core

Carol Thomas

The soft centre and I plunge my thumb into the golden rind of the tangerine. The pungent aromatic scent takes me back to brilliant blue skies which turned to gold in January evenings. My childhood memories are full of warmth and happiness and caring people. Not for me the deprived and disaffected childhood. I remember being happy – intensely so. I even loved the rain which came after the dry tangerine season. I would stand at the window pressing my forehead on the cool glass and watch the huge drops outside. A tropical rainstorm can wreak havoc in the garden. It can be sudden and total. You would be drenched even with an umbrella.

Perhaps I loved those rainstorms because we didn't have to go to school. And because there were six of us at home we would play games, mostly hide and seek appropriate in dark rooms – dark because the wooden 'Demerara' windows and the jalousies were closed.

There were occasions that I liked even better. Stories were my favourite times. My mother tells of my being about 3 years old, demanding a story whatever happened, nor would I go to bed without one. Before I could read myself there was a serial of 'Tiny Tim' based on the Dickens story which was run for children in the evening newspaper. I would follow my mother around, newspaper in hand, until she could find time to read it. Once I could read, I would leave the rainy-day games to find a spot where I could be on my own to read. 'Selfish', my father called it, and he would sometimes come and send me off to join the others.

We had help in the house, and I remember what vivid story-tellers they were. None of this 'book' reading, but real vivid stories told in Biblical language, enthralling us for hours. We were spellbound.

Later when I could climb the mango tree I stuck my book under my blouse and by the time I reached the highest sturdy branch I could see over the roof tops to the sea far away in the distance. I was inaccessible there and could read to my heart's content.

The house was often filled with music, for by the time I was born my eldest sister was playing Bach and Schumann and Beethoven. There were many friends, and people of every race would come and go. Nor should you imagine that there were never things to cloud the horizon. Childhood is too unsure, too tenuous, too coming-to-understand for that. But my future was beginning to take shape. That eldest sister was to be the musician. I was to become a librarian. But I'm rushing ahead.

Part of my childhood was during the Second World War. Back at home we knew little of the real wartime experiences. But we were British, and sent soldiers and airmen as well as recruits to join up and fight in the British forces. We knew many families who lost brothers or sisters. Troops were stationed on our island and my parents often entertained the young men at our home. My father was an air raid warden and I remember mock air raid warnings when we turned off the lights and told jokes and stories in the dark. I'm ashamed to say these were happy and exciting times.

One interesting aspect of the war was the migration of refugees to our island. I remember at school a Jewish Russian family of children. The girl sat next to me. She had beautiful reddish golden hair. We became very good friends, and she used to tell me about the Jewish festivals and ritual. There were many other Eastern European families trying to escape from the brutalities of the war front. We made them welcome, and those who stayed always remained our friends.

And so my childhood and adolescence ended. I grew up. I went off to train as a librarian. Having during my youth swallowed the combination of fairy-tale and Christian ethic, I was under the impression that I'd marry and live happily ever after. I expected to play the traditional supporting role as wife. However, in order to have anything except the bare necessities it was essential for me to work. I was very interested in librarianship, and I only gave up when my babies arrived. They were my responsibility as I saw it and my husband never had a sleepless night.

At that time I used to review books, and one I received was Betty Friedan's *The Natural Superiority of Women*. It confirmed for me ideas which had been growing in my mind – that women have a strength and endurance which gives us advantages, if only because we are going to bear the babies and would need that strength. I didn't actually believe that women were superior – that wasn't the point. I believed that as human beings we are a very fine race and that we have different strengths from men. It helped me to a feeling that women need never accept an inferior role. Difference does not imply deficiency. In the face of the way the world, and the society in which I lived, was going at that time, this was a positive way of seeing women. Before then I had not thought of myself as strong. It was a bit of a shock to me, and an even greater one to recognise that I had a strong inner core. I'd always thought of myself as easy-going. However, it was a long time before I took on the responsibility of that strength, and I am still coming to terms with that understanding.

By 1962 the University of the West Indies extended its faculty of Arts and Sciences within the Caribbean islands. The earliest faculties had been established by the 1950s in Jamaica and the plan was to set up various departments in several of the

Caribbean islands. By this time I had realised that if I was to survive as a person I would have to make my own life. A chance to be with my children and go to university seemed a step that would achieve just that. I used the money I had saved from my part-time jobs partly to finance myself, and enrolled as an undergraduate. I spent the next three years reading English, and I loved it.

The children were at school all day, and I had help in the house. But it was hard work, and long hours, often starting at eight in the morning. Then I'd have to see to the children and help with the housework when I got home – all the things family life demands — so that by the time the last child had gone to bed, I'd be exhausted. I would often go to bed then too, at nine o'clock, and get up at 2 a.m. to study. If I had a paper to write or a seminar to participate in, I would see the sun rise and then be ready for lectures at 8. It never seriously occurred to me that I should give it up.

All this time I thought that perhaps a better relationship might develop with my husband, but it didn't. There were times when misery would get the better of me and I'd sit staring at my books, my eyes running along the lines of print without my knowing a word of what I had read. There were times when I plotted suicide – yes, seriously – and there were others when rage and resentment ate at my very being.

I suppose I had received at school what was a very traditional education. I only realised how one-sided it was when at university one of the required subjects was Caribbean History. I remember the shock at discovering that I had a very sketchy knowledge of the past history of the West Indies. When the true brutality of the slave trade was told, my fellow students were angry to the point of rebellion at discovering important historical aspects of the subjugation of Black Peoples. 'Why have we not been told before? Why has our history been concealed from us?'

I was rather more prepared for it, because I had read Eric

Williams's *Capitalism and Slavery* in which he proposes that slavery had not been abolished because of human enlightenment or for humanitarian reasons, but because of economic factors: it was simply no longer financially worthwhile to buy and sell slaves, as his research proves.

After I graduated, I found that there were no jobs in librarianship, and, although anxious about it, took a job in a secondary school. I loved it – the headmaster hadn't come across someone who actually felt passionate about teaching English. I quickly grew to enjoy my pupils. I'd been hesitant about the rather large young men there who had a reputation as trouble makers. Of course there were disasters when I hadn't prepared properly, but I learnt to make things as interesting as possible, and to convey my enthusiasm to the class. However, I knew that if I was going to stay in teaching, I'd need a professional qualification.

I could go abroad and take a diploma. The children? I investigated with my parents. They would keep them for a year. After much confusion and heart searching, I set out to take the course in England. I knew I was determined to make an escape from a very difficult domestic scene. I was sorry I could not be straightforward about it before I left, but I knew my parents would never be a party to my plans. I could not talk about my marriage to them. I'd tried, but they'd made it impossible. And it would have been an impossible burden for them to bear. People have said it was very brave of me to come here to live: in fact, it would have been impossible for me to stay. Was I a coward to come? I was not really strong enough to take on the world of my little island.

So I came to Britain. Yet again, I hardly know how I passed through the exams. I felt so unhappy at leaving my children and family! But to see all my husband's accusations on paper were enough to prevent thoughts of returning, because he made trouble amongst my family and friends. To feel that my parents and friends condemned me was even more bitter, and my greatest fear was that I would not have my children with me.

When I was a child I didn't know anyone who was divorced. And when the grown ups I loved mentioned such a state, it was with tremendous moral disapproval, like some of the other things they regarded as 'illicit relationships'. In the 'respectable' middle class, with a background of slavery only 150 years before, there were those who held on to appearances of middle class morals with tremendous tenacity. Behind the façade existed a certain sexual licence. This is the reality of Victorian morality. Now I too was to become divorced.

I remember the feeling of total isolation. When the actual case came to be heard I did not even tell my sons, then 16 and 12, and over here with me. I was filled with thoughts that anyone who knew would disapprove and despise me, afraid that it would affect my job or my reputation as a teacher, and I did not want to involve them in my fears and anxieties. I remember hugging the fences as I walked along, expressing my shame and fear, I suppose, by trying to disappear into the privet as I slunk along those streets.

I went on with my teaching – that was one thing I felt happy about. I tried to make friends, and to go out on my own. I had not realised it before: a woman didn't go out alone back home. At least, I can't think of a time when I'd ever done so. All the 'important' decisions had been made first by my father and then my husband. We are hopefully moving from that now, but there is a generation like me who are caught between what we have been socialised to accept and what the contemporary world demands.

Teaching in London had many surprises for me. The immediate one was the sophistication of London teenagers. Pupils in my small island seemed simple and easy to manage by comparison. I was appalled at the cynicism of both pupils and teachers towards education. Teachers seemed to have grown to expect poor results, while pupils and families had no idea how to achieve success. It was obvious from the start that Black children were at the bottom of the pile. I kept thinking, as the old saying goes, there but for the grace of God (whatever that means) went I and mine.

It seemed to me that the white working class, at least, had a strong supporting network. The children of Black parents then had all the disadvantages of the oppressed and the poor, without that support network. They still lack a positive designated place in an intransigent society. Moreover they are disadvantaged and oppressed by the very institutions which are there to help.

I found out very painfully a bit of what its like to be disadvantaged when I looked for lodgings, and again when I eventually tried to buy my own home. 'Don't try here,' they would say, 'try . . .' and they would name the nearest deprived street. Or when I arrived at the door, 'Sorry, the flat has just been taken.' I know that flat-hunting can be depressing, but for me it seemed soul-destroying. Gradually I had come to terms with being the foreigner. I had to learn to ignore the mask that would drop over the smiling features of a shop assistant. Thank goodness for the friends that one makes in spite of the rejections.

I worry about my sister, a few years older than me, who has had a traumatic experience in the break-up of her marriage. She has lost every emotional and economic resource she could have expected just as she faces old age. And this is through none of her own doing, since her husband squandered every penny they possessed. She clings to the dream that another man will come along and provide all she expected and moreover felt was her due. Her notion of happiness and self-fulfilment, even after all her husband has put her through, depends on having a man looking after her and providing her security.

Because she is untrained, her wages are pitiable. She has many tremendous qualities. Although she is 60 she cannot afford to retire, because her husband paid no stamps and she will get no pension. We women need so badly to make ourselves economically viable, and to keep ourselves informed of our choices. Had my sister taken some training after the children were old enough, her situation now would still have been traumatic but she would have had the assurance that she was equipped to be independent.

I didn't come to teaching until I was 38 – the middle of my life. Nowadays the job that I do is a tremendous challenge. I am in that branch of education which has come to be known as multi-cultural education. It is a privilege for me because I believe it points the way forward for all education. Am I evangelical? No, because this is not a matter of faith. It is a matter of rationality, and if there are any parallels with religion they begin and end with a passionate conviction.

There has never been a justification for an education that is highly selective, biased, elitist and ethnocentric. It seems that English education has gradually if unconsciously grown from roots fed by notions of superiority. Every choice we as teachers make contributes to a child's sense of reality. If we fail to tell the major facts of any issue we limit their understanding. If we fail to put learning into the context of society as a whole we narrow the child's perception of her relevance. And if we fail to give a pupil the skill she needs to survive in society we waste her time. If you thought multi-cultural education was to teach Black children about their history you are a little short of the truth. It is for all pupils. It sets out to broaden the understanding of both teachers and pupils and to counter racism.

The industrial West often acts as if knowledge descended from on high and pretends that a technological society was created out of its natural superiority. In fact most of modern Western thought is firmly based on and derived from societies which enjoyed a highly developed civilisation, stability and economy long before Europeans developed theirs. Indeed, the Renaissance could not have occurred without these former cultures. The Chinese were responsible for inventions like the magnetic compass, the rudder, quantitative cartology and mechanical clockwork. Modern computers could not operate without the concept of 'O' derived from the Hindus. Our mathematical and astronomical knowledge comes from the Arabs. If we pride ourselves on Western industrial progress, we must give respect where it is due. We must stop acting as if science was born here. Who were the Black scientists, and where are they now? Why were they ignored?

Teachers must learn to broaden their own outlook on the world. Human beings are inventive: why are we then having so much difficulty in producing Black graduate scientists from our schools? Is it possible we are not engaging the attention and interest of Black pupils because it is assumed by white teachers that they are only good at physical things? And does this influence Black pupils' assumptions about what they can and can't do? I'm certain it does. A destructive racism exists in society and we have to ensure that the school pays attention to racism's implications of power and does what it can to counter the offensiveness of racism to human sensibility. The time has come when we can no longer hide behind ignorance: if any group is singled out for a particular oppression, there is going to be trouble.

It is an indictment of the education system here that Black groups have sometimes chosen to open their own schools. There is no religious principle involved. There is no feeling that their children will do better without the distractions of the opposite sex. It is simply that they feel schools are failing their children and adversely affecting their chances. They want to give their children the skills that are the right of every child who goes to school. Moreover they often feel that attempts at multi-cultural education have been misguided, as indeed they sometimes have. They are suspicious of the encouragement of 'dialect' in the classroom, as well they might be, for they know that the powerful in this country use only Standard English. Where multi-cultural education in a school has meant only a steel band, a Divali celebration, or a few chappatis shared in the classroom, who has benefited? And of what relevance is this to an understanding of how power is distributed around the world?

It's natural that parents of Black children have looked for the return of the three Rs as being crucial for their children. But we need to do even more than provide the basic skills.

The presence of large numbers of children from ethnic minorities pressed the authorities to do something to 'cope' with their needs. Often this meant 'teach them English and they will become assimilated'. It soon became apparent that this did not work. Basic changes were needed across the whole curriculum. Assimilation into a society that had already decided Black was inferior was not, in any case, a suitable aim.

Now my life is changing again. My boys have grown up, and I live on my own – what bliss! I thought I'd be tremendously lonely but there is always so much to do. My father did say I was selfish! The flat is often full of family and friends. I'm sure I have the occasional mope especially when I look in the mirror and realise that being fat and grey-haired hasn't been fashionable for a long time. What I really must consider is what I am going to do with the rest of my life. There is still so much that I don't know, so many books to read. I've many friends of different ages, races, and both genders. I have women friends with whom I share so much and feel so at ease. I have men friends too. I think I understand them better, and feel more relaxed with them, than I did when I was younger. Black people also need to have each other if only to reaffirm ourselves and to support each other. Race itself is rather a superficial quality, for there is always diversity within a group. However it is the common heritage, the shared experience and the deeper assumptions we have learned about ourselves and each other which are crucial for us.

Now I ask myself: shall I live with my special man friend? I can't call him boy friend, since we are no longer young. It would seem a loss of the independence I now enjoy. I am fortunate in many ways to have a caring companion. Statistics show that in the older age group there are fewer men than women, and in any case perhaps it becomes harder to find someone who shares your interests when you are older?

Shall I take early retirement? And let a younger and perhaps more energetic person have a go at my job? Can I afford that financial indulgence? I came to Britain late, and won't receive much of a pension from teaching, and none from the state. In any case, I never want to be dependent on the state. I'm making plans to get more financially secure. And I'm taking care that I'll *always* have something interesting to do.

CHAPTER 15

Question Everything!

Lucy Gray

Recently in London there was an exhibition organised by some women called 'Exploring Living Memory'. It was a collection of photographs, newspaper cuttings, memorabilia of various kinds, depicting the lives of ordinary people, and events that have shaped those lives. I went to see it twice, and spent a long time gazing at old sepia-tinted snaps of people I had never known, but who none the less looked very familiar to me.

This feeling of recognition surprised, even shocked me, because at the same time everything looked so strange, as if it were not me, but someone else I knew who had lived through those times, worn those clothes, lived in those terraced houses. I did not recognise myself. Most women suffer from a lack of identity, whether they realise it or not. Many of them are prepared to accept the identity given to them of daughter, sister, wife, mother, but if they do not, the world can be a very lonely place. I hardly think about the past at all. It does not seem to belong to me, as I am now.

I was born in the north of England, the only child of parents who both came from very large, poor families. My father was in the regular army, and when I was small we moved around the country from one furnished room to another. It must have been hard for my mother, I remember her saying that soldiers had a bad reputation in the 1920s, and people didn't want them in their homes. For this reason I was always enjoined to 'be a good girl and don't make a noise'. My father would have liked a son, but having to be content with me, made sure I was brought up as a soldier's daughter – speak when you're spoken to, do as you're bid, stiff upper lip and no tears. It marked me for life. Instead of emotional release I get indigestion, nervous tension and back pain! When I started school my father went abroad, and we did not have a home of our own until he came back for good and I was by that time at grammar school. From being a shadowy figure thousands of miles away, he was once more a physical presence in uniform, whose boots had to be unlaced each night and puttees removed, neatly rolled ready for the next morning.

We moved to the south of England when I was 12, and I transferred to a co-educational grammar school. I was always being urged by my parents to work hard and get a good education. However, they didn't like it when I got it, because it made me want to change things. We had a history mistress who made a deep impression on me. This was during the 1930s and Hitler's rise to power. Her husband had been gassed in the trenches in the First World War and she encouraged us to think about what was happening in Europe. I remember there was one boy in those debates who always argued for the Nazis, and another for the Communists. Meanwhile the girls said nothing at all. The message that reached me was from neither camp but from the teacher, who urged us to accept nothing, question everything, and I have tried to follow that precept ever since.

There was very little career guidance for girls in my school. The only option after university seemed to be the teaching profession. After the Munich crisis, war looked inevitable and in fact started when I was 17. I left school and went into the Civil Service. At work I found myself among a group of young men who were very politically conscious. Some were pacifists, some Communists. One of them, whom I later married, volunteered for the RAF the day after Germany invaded Russia. He was killed one month after we were married, in what Mr Churchill boasted was a show of strength to the enemy: the one thousand bomber raids. In fact they were a tragic waste of aircrews, some not fully trained, and of aircraft, and achieved very little. My politics then, and since, were very radical, and this caused some trouble at home. My parents were staunch working-class Tory, and I can understand that now. They were afraid of change, afraid of losing what they had managed to achieve, a much more comfortable life than their parents had.

The town we lived in was blitzed, and as we were on war work the department was moved to the comparative calm of Surrey, just outside London. There I was drawn into a Marxist group led by some refugees from northern Europe. I went to several meetings but was really in no mood for didactics, suffering from a reaction to the death of my husband and all the waste I saw around me. I spent the rest of the war having a good time in London.

The relationships I formed during that time were very superficial and I could never take any of them seriously. I suppose I was promiscuous, but it was quite in keeping with the times. But I was still very conditioned in my social behaviour, if not my politics, and as soon as the war was over got engaged to a man of the same nationality, the same class, the same background – in other words a perfectly acceptable match. The courtship was very assiduous, flowers, notes, gifts . . . but the disillusion set in very soon after the wedding. In those days, however, and with that background, women made the best of their situations. Divorce was simply not an option open to them except under certain extreme conditions, and a state of chronic dissatisfaction and unhappiness was not one of them! I was soon made to realise that I existed solely as the property of my husband. His will in everything overruled mine, and this extended of course to the children. I have a daughter and two sons. The first birth was a difficult one, and the maternity hospital a nightmare. The two male doctors treated the women abominably, showing their masculine contempt quite openly.

Motherhood did not come naturally to me I'm afraid. I can still recall the terrible boredom and frustration of being at home with two toddlers in a town where I knew very few people, and where there was no relief of any kind from the feeling of isolation. Add to that the post-war conditions of food shortages, poor housing and not much money, and it's not surprising that after the birth of my second child I suffered from post-natal depression, though I didn't realise it was that at the time. This was at the height of the 'cold war' in the early 1950s and I felt totally bleak about the future. It was almost like a physical presence, something large and threatening looming just behind my shoulder. There was no one I could talk to about it. I have never regretted having the children. I do regret not being more openly loving to them when they were very small.

After the third baby I was determined not to have any more. I was in an economic trap, totally dependent on my husband and his moods, and the only way out of that trap was to get a job. As long as I had small children to look after that was out of the question. I started to take typing and shorthand at evening class thinking that would be the only part-time work I was likely to find. In the event I got a job in the accounts department of a large organisation and stayed with them for over 20 years.

Two years after my father retired, my mother had a very severe heart attack. I've wondered recently whether those two events were connected. The first news I had was that she was not expected to recover and it had a shattering effect on me. She was 65, but I had never thought about her being old, let alone dying. About this time also things started to get really bad at home. As the children reached adolescence my husband got more and more domineering, and though my daughter played the submissive role expected of her, the older boy tried to assert himself and rows with his father increased. Quite often these were deliberately provoked by my husband, in order to prove his superiority and demonstrate his power over us. We lived under the constant threat of his disapproval and bad temper. He had a very loud cutting voice and an overbearing physical manner. We all felt as if we were being watched and this drew the children closer to me. They only felt safe talking about anything when he was not there.

It was like a conspiracy. It resulted also in separating the children from one another and had a particularly bad effect on the youngest child, who became completely isolated both within the family and outside it. I sometimes wonder how I could have lessened the impact on him, but events seemed to have a momentum of their own and there was nothing I could do to stop them. During these years I had gradually taken on more work, with more responsibility, and more money. My husband enjoyed the fact that I was bringing in more money, but got increasingly resentful of my success. I was not allowed to talk about my work at all, whereas he did nothing but complain about his.

Fortunately I was able to separate my job and my home. I felt fine at work, and dreadful at home. I had all the classic symptoms of depression, and was taking large doses of Librium as well as sleeping pills. After insisting on buying twin beds I found I could not even sleep in the same room as my husband, and slept on the sofa downstairs. By this time I think he began to get frightened that I might leave. It had not really occurred to him before that I might actually do that, although I had warned him many times that I could not continue to live in that way.

For some time I had been paying from my earnings for the family food, my clothes and the children's, and making up my daughter's grant. He paid the mortgage and overheads. I was still able to save quite a bit though, and hoped to have enough to leave by the time my youngest child had finished 'O' levels. My daughter never came back home to live after university. She had been physically attacked twice by her father after violent arguments. The older boy had been literally locked out of the house, with all his possessions, so the situation was drawing to its inevitable conclusion. I found a flat and moved out, with my youngest son. It took a long time though before we all managed to recover and put the pieces together again. I was anxious about my older two, who at first set themselves up in difficult and unsuccessful relationships. Meanwhile the younger boy talked to me a lot about suicide and I was very worried about him indeed. He had immersed himself completely in his studies, and passed the Cambridge entrance. While he was waiting to go up he got a temporary job with a young high flyer in the City and that at last helped to crack the shell.

I had vowed not to take any more pills after I left, and I kept to that. The first few months of reaction and adjustment were very hard and though I had a close woman friend at work, she had her own problems at this time, and there was no one else I could talk to. In desperation I went to the Marriage Guidance Council, and once a week for a couple of months I simply went along and talked and cried it out of my system. The counsellor was very good and once she realised that was all she could do for me, just sat and listened.

As well as the emotional problems there were the financial and legal ones. My husband would not agree to a divorce and I could not afford to wait five or six years before getting some kind of settlement of the matrimonial home, so I took an action under the Married Woman's Property Act. This act dates back to 1882 and I had to produce substantial evidence proving my contribution to the original deposit (25 years before) and to the general household expenses since that time. My husband was obstructive, discharging two different solicitors and obtaining delays. His whole attitude was based on his proprietorial rights, and they of course included me. My solicitors were grossly inefficient, and I seemed to be doing most of the donkey work myself. Eventually, three years later, a date was fixed for the hearing in the Family Division of the High Court and I turned up to find my husband was conducting his own case and would be cross-examining me. But at the end of it all I won my case and half the value of the house and its contents, with six months' grace for my husband to arrange his affairs. He was absolutely furious and said he wanted a divorce as soon as possible. I replied I wanted that three years ago. My QC thought it a very good result – on the basis of a recent judgment he expected I would get only one third. What everyone seemed to overlook was that I had been paying rent on a furnished flat all this time, as well as supporting my son, while my husband had been living rent free – the house was paid for. I was awarded costs, but didn't realise this meant court costs only. I still had to pay my own solicitor's bill which was out of all proportion to the work they had done. I was by then tired of the whole thing and just wanted to forget it.

Came the wonderful day when I was able to move into my own house, by myself. It didn't last long. Dad had been living alone since Mum died, with frequent visits from me to stock the larder, cook, and provide him with a bit of company. At a distance of 300 miles this was no joke, especially on top of a full-time job, and driving back one weekend I had a nasty accident. I could see in any case that he was sliding downhill. He had very few contacts and made no effort to get involved in any activities. So he came to live with me and is still here.

I retired from work two years ago, having reached a position I had never imagined possible. The organisation used to be very patriarchal, to the extent that one or two jobs being done by women had been officially classed as 'female supervisory'. The skills required were no different from those needed for many other jobs done by men, but the pay was lower. By a series of chances I filled one of those jobs, and soon after achieved equal pay. Further promotions after that meant that I was able to retire at 60 with enough to live on. Had I been a man retiring on the same rate of pay of course my pension would have been much higher. Most women with children returning to pensionable employment suffer through those lost years, and indeed the whole tax and social security system discriminates against women.

My father is now suffering from senile dementia. Physically he is quite fit, eats a lot and sleeps a lot, but is becoming incapable of rational thought, and can do quite irrational, even dangerous things if left alone. My head tells me this is a medical condition, my heart says that it is one more manifestation of patriarchal oppression. I now do voluntary work for Shelter two days a week and for *Spare Rib* magazine on another day. I belong to the Older Feminist Network and do as much in that as I can.

It seems to me as I am writing this that the past twenty years of my life reflect the rise of the women's movement, its achievements and its limitations. We have a long way to go before women are freed from the social conditioning that traps them in all kinds of oppressive situations. Is the movement running out of steam? Why don't more women take an active interest in the issues that affect their lives so crucially? Are we going to have to join the men in their political power games before we can become an effective force? I have yet to discover any real sense of purpose in the movement. Perhaps I feel this urgency in myself because I am getting older and time is running out for me. I see my daughter now in another form of trap. She has been married for ten years and on the pill all that time. She has an interesting job, and until the last few years was not bothered about having children. Her husband was definitely against it. At some point though she realised she didn't want to stay childless all her life and eventually managed to persuade her husband. She had no trouble getting pregnant, but the baby was born at six months and died after three days. Since then she has had some cancerous tissue removed from the cervix and although the doctor says this should not make it impossible, she has not become pregnant again. I do not think the pill was such a good thing for women. It was pushed on to them by the medical fraternity without any long-term trials because it released men from any responsibility for contraception. If men had been asked to take regular doses of a chemical hormone there would have been an uproar.

I used to think that after retirement I ought to become more active in politics. The way this country is being changed into a right-wing authoritarian state is a catastrophe, and anyone who thinks that should plainly attempt to do something about it. The thought of getting entangled in any of the political parties with their male power structure appeals to me less and less. I would prefer to join other women in some kind of political grouping of the peace, ecological and feminist movements if that were possible. It's always been hard for me to make decisions affecting my own life, and my attitude towards the future is very ambivalent. On the one hand I feel an urge to get really involved in some form of protest, and on the other I would just like to get as far away as possible and spend the rest of my life on some sunny shore with a good book. At the moment I really can't do either.

CHAPTER 16

'But How Did You Get Out?'

Esther Mayer

I came to England from Vienna just after my tenth birthday in July 1939. My father was a lawyer, and one day he stood up in court and said that under a dictatorship, sedition was not a crime. He was arrested the same day, imprisoned for six weeks, and given a month to get out of the country, with the threat of a concentration camp if he didn't.

I came over here with both my parents. We had a job getting out of Austria, but this was not nearly as difficult as getting into England. The Germans wanted to get rid of the Jews: England didn't want us. I still remember my amazement at people here asking us, 'But how did you get out?' I thought, 'How can these grown-ups not understand what this is all about?' From 4 years of age I'd heard about Hitler and the threat to the Jews, and most of the people I knew had spent the last two years queueing and scrabbling for visas and affidavits and permits to get out.

I spent the first couple of years here just being amazed by the different culture. I couldn't believe that English children didn't know about the Spanish Civil War and the Abyssinian War. I'd grown up with them. It was very hard to accept that I'd come to a country where no one seemed to understand anything about me or my family. In Austria my parents had mixed only with other Jews. When we came to England we were without family. We followed my father around the Midlands. First he was interned and then he joined the Pioneer Corps while my mother became a cook. I didn't meet another Jewish person all through the rest of my childhood. I didn't experience blatant anti-semitism at school, just ignorance, a total disregard which felt different from the open hostility I'd known in Austria but didn't feel comfortable either.

As I became more confident, I dared to be different, and enjoyed school. I was rebellious there, always in trouble, very conscious of not being able to rebel at home because of my parents' loss and distress. When the war ended, I went off to drama school in London. I felt so green! All those young people were so sophisticated to my mind, smoking, drinking, wearing make-up and clued up about things I'd never heard of. I worked very hard and took it all seriously. Later, I loved working in provincial repertory companies, but after, when I had the children, the theatre didn't seem so important any more. When I tried to get jobs in London I wasn't very successful.

During my teens I used to fall madly in love at a distance: first with my English teacher, a woman I'm still in touch with, and then with a whole series of male teachers. At 22 I fell in love with my husband, who was also in the theatre. I never doubted that his career was more important than mine. He wasn't Jewish. My parents would have preferred him to be, but emigration had put things in perspective for them, and they were able to accept things which would have horrified them in their earlier days. At first it wasn't a problem for me either. But later I became aware of a whole set of problems around being Jewish, and tried to make him aware too. He didn't deal with my Jewishness by resisting it in me, but by wanting to make a documentary about Jews. He read and learnt more about being Jewish than I'd ever known. My fear of being taken over in this way was always a point of conflict between us.

The marriage had many positive aspects. We were close, and for the most part it was an honest relationship. It was also very exclusive, something which gave us strengths when we were younger, but turned into constraints as we grew older. We both enjoyed having children, looking after the babies, watching them grow up: those were good years.

The children didn't have any religious education from us. Looking back, I think we presented them with a Jewish cultural background. My husband's family were not a part of our lives: he didn't include them. My parents, however, were always involved, and the children grew up knowing what had happened and why we were here. When my elder daughter was at primary school she came home one day and said a little boy had called her a 'bloody Jew'. Both my daughters became aware early on of what being Jewish meant.

I didn't consciously model my marriage on my parents', but it was the only model I had of something that had survived. I think I had a desperate need to copy it – for continuing, surviving. I was also very conscious of being an only child. I remember always hoping I'd meet somebody I could marry and 'get it over soon', settle it, because I had to do it, there seemed no choice. But what if there wasn't anybody? I was scared. So I was very ready to fall in love and reproduce what my parents had. But the seeds of the ending of my marriage were there in the beginning. Even in the early days, whether it was premonition or what, my husband found it very hard to tolerate my women friends. I'd have to arrange to meet them on the night he was working or going away. We could entertain other couples, but it was always difficult with my women friends.

It was not really until I left the theatre and went back to college that I began to think about independence. First I had been very dependent as a child, then a dependent wife, then my children were dependent on me – and then my parents, too, became dependent on me. I began to plot out my pieces of territory, as it were, and realised I didn't have any. I began to push for space and time, mark out for myself emotional and intellectual areas to do with my work and my friends, some of them women and men I'd become very close to at college. This in itself didn't threaten the marriage, but it loosened it, for both of us. As I began to stretch one way, so my husband would stretch in another direction, and this would enable me to make yet another move. Although there was a lot of jockeying for position, our relationship had lasted for a long time, and neither of us wanted to disrupt it.

Once I'd qualified and begun work my husband was, as far as he could be, very supportive. He encouraged me, he got the children up, he cooked and he cleaned – as long as it fitted in with his own work. It seemed an equal partnership, but my discontent was rooted in the knowledge that the equality was on his terms. I felt he defended himself against the freedom I was getting, especially the close friends I'd made, by trying again to incorporate the area of my work into his own, just as he had done with my Jewish identity.

I know that the problems I encountered in my marriage many married women would count themselves lucky to have in comparison. I wasn't ill-treated or abused in any way. Most people saw ours as the ideal marriage. We were always together, we supported each other, shared the same kinds of ideas. When I wanted to break from it I used to feel incredibly guilty, wondering what I was making all the fuss about. The push to separate came from me. The children were grown up and I hoped they would survive unharmed. During the last three years of my marriage it got to the point where every night on my way home from work I'd think, 'I can't go on doing this for ever, but I'll think about it another day. Tonight I've got to get home and get the supper.' Finally it got to the day when I did think about it, and knew for sure I couldn't contemplate staying married for the rest of my life.

By that time I had met a woman I did want to share my life with. Meeting her helped to make me realise that there were other possibilities, but I like to think that she wasn't the reason for my getting out of the marriage. I'm quite sure that if it hadn't been that, something else would have happened. I might have gone to Israel to live on a kibbutz; it was always at the back of my mind. I suppose that if we had gone as a family when the children were young, life would have been different, and so would the marriage. But it was the one thing my husband would not do. He was not the sort of person to want to live on a kibbutz and he didn't have any real links with Israel.

During my marriage I had chosen to remain 'faithful', chosen to be exclusive. For twenty-five years I signalled that I wasn't available for other relationships. However, I think that long before I met someone else I began to make myself available. But what happened was astounding. It was something I had never, never considered. I'd always had close relationships with women, and always enjoyed women's company. But I was astonished when I realised I was making a very deep and sexual relationship with a woman. I was delighted. I thought it was marvellous and I still do. It's been a most easy, straightforward way of living. After being married for so long, it feels stress-free, joyful. It was wretched trying to tell my husband and I didn't really know how to do it. I was ashamed of myself because I seemed to be behaving like a wilful spoilt child, having to have my way in spite of everybody. It was too hard for me to convey to anybody that a marriage doesn't have to be disastrous to be impossible.

I discovered how good it is to love a woman as I went along. It is only with a woman that I have discovered real mutuality and sharing, a sharing that never needs discussion and has no restraining strings attached. Even with the most mundane chores, we both see what needs doing and it gets done. It's so easy!

My daughters are wonderful. I love them. When I began this relationship they were 19 and 21. I told my elder daughter early on, and she was as supportive and understanding as I'd hoped she would be, and I was very grateful for that. However, when she herself came out as a lesbian it made for difficulties between us for although she had none of the conventional problems in coming out to her mother, it made it more difficult for her to express any anger or upset about her parents' divorce. My younger daughter was horrified to begin with. It took her a long time to accept, and it goes on being difficult for her in some ways. But she has come from a point of horror to one of compassion and tolerance.

As a young child I had been comparatively politically aware, but by the time I left school I'd become apolitical and even mindless. I don't think I questioned much until I was in my 30s. Then I came into contact with the issues around apartheid, which I learnt about through meeting with South African refugees. Nowadays I dabble in a lot of movements, though I don't easily commit myself to any of them. I have a great interest in and sympathy for the women's movement, although I have to struggle with separatist ideas. I do understand that we have to get together and sort ourselves out first, but I suppose generally in life I go for reform rather than for revolution. I'm involved in all the usual kind of middle-class causes, like CND, Friends of the Earth and Oxfam. I pay my dues, read the newsletters, send donations: as I said, I dabble.

I can see that I am an older woman now. I don't feel older though. I've just discovered ageism. I'm still working, and I suppose I can go on doing what I do for as long as I choose. Through my work I have seen more clearly the roles women are forced into in heterosexual relationships, but when it was happening to me I didn't perceive it. The women's movement didn't seem relevant to me to begin with. I wanted to stay at home to look after the children. I didn't feel I would rather be doing something else, and I felt at least equal to the men I knew. It took me twenty-five years to understand I wasn't, to understand where the power was, and what the complications were for me. Looking back on it I can see that there were always struggles going on about who was doing the most valuable and valued thing.

My feelings towards Israel are now quite unreasonable. The political situation there is horrific, and yet I remain committed to the country. I see it as a cause, and I'm more committed to Israel than to any other cause. If it was feasible I'd still want to live there. But not on my own. When my lover and I retire, if they'd take a couple of hardworking women in their 60s, and she wanted to go, yes, I'd still like to go.

CHAPTER 17

Who Feels It, Knows It

Maria Benjamin

In the 1920s and 1930s there were very few Black women here. They came to England in larger numbers twenty or more years later. There were many Black men here though. They'd come in two main ways, either as seamen, or to fight in the British army. There were numbers of Black seamen in the ports like Liverpool, Cardiff and Hull, and in the docklands of Manchester. In places like these today there are lots of older Black men.

English women have a bad name as far as Black men are concerned, because they were the ones to look down on the Black people more. Black men would therefore look for an Irish, Scottish or Welsh wife. If you see an older Black man with a white wife, she is likely to be one of these. Black men looked to these women because they'd also suffered in their histories with the English, and there was some kind of shared experience between them. I was born in Liverpool: my father is Jamaican and my mother is Italian.

We need to look at white people's perspective of what Black people are. During that period, when many Black men married white women, they produced mixed-race children who could 'pass', often as Italians or other dark-skinned people. This meant that often white people didn't recognise Black children as Black in that period. If you look, for example, into the history of the youth work movement, you'll get older white women claiming they never worked with any Black girls. They didn't recognise us – and in any case, the emphasis was on us trying to blend in.

It is harder for mixed-race people. The line we tread is so hard, and so easy to fall off. At school I only needed to have one row with my white friends, and that was it! Black men and women know exactly where they stand, but mixed-race are never totally accepted as whole people. By whole I mean you're not accepted as white by white people, nor as Black by Black people. You have to make a choice: every mixed-race person goes through it. You want to be accepted by Black people desperately more than you do by whites. Race is not just skin, it's a state of mind. You have to follow up your choice: you must be seen to be making that commitment to Black people. You can dress more Black, use the language, which is so important, and you can listen to the music, which is the politics. Black music is about the pain in life, and about what is going on for Black people. Even if you don't read the Black newspapers, you'll hear from the music what the government is doing, who's been killed, and all the local news.

When I was young, the feeling in our families was that we should just put up with racism for a quiet life, try to blend in or be more acceptable. It wasn't that we didn't experience racism. When I see kids today who just don't stand for it, I feel proud. They're going to make the changes.

I got used to racism as a child, but I never accepted it. So I was labelled stubborn and difficult, as having 'a chip on my shoulder'. My father always reminded me that white people would have no good thoughts about me because in their view I'd only be good for certain things, like sport and dancing. White people could never think we were as good as them, and could achieve the same things. Eventually he'd let me go out to the youth club, but only once a month. He'd say, 'The white man has got you in school all day, you should be with me at night, otherwise you'll have no culture.' At school I was getting picked to do sports and nothing else. This happens nowadays too to

Black kids. I was good at other subjects, especially English and Maths, but the teachers would always put me down when I knew the answers. They would say, 'It's always you sticking your hand up.' I felt they hated it, me sticking up my hand, and they thought I should hold back, wait, giving them a chance to humiliate me. I was a very good runner, and at 14 I was the inter-schools Victor Ludorum (winner of the games), which is very unusual, as you would normally be older to win it. My dad wasn't even pleased because he thought I was living up to white people's expectations of Black people. He didn't encourage my sisters to play sports. He took every opportunity to stop me practising and competing. He wanted me to be good at the things white people didn't expect us to be good at. Our white neighbours were amazed that we had piano lessons!

I have earlier memories of racism. When I was about 7 I used to take bottles back to the shop and a white woman offered me a penny to show her my tail. In those days many white people believed Black people had the stump of a tail left over from when we were monkeys. I didn't know what she meant, grabbed the bottle and ran back to my yard. When I was in the convent school the nuns would put three girls in a bath with three inches of water in it. But I was never allowed to have anyone in the bath with me. The nuns would put Omo in the water and scrub me all over with nail brushes to make me white. I could never bring myself to use that washing powder. I don't feel bitter about it, but I do feel sad that I didn't have the words to handle it at the time. But I would always tell them that Christ was not white. The first page of the Bible shows that. He was made from dust and I've never seen white dust. Even their religion is racist. Because I never went to school with other Black kids, I used to think I was unique, but the nuns were always so derogatory. Souls rush to soul-mates, and my first friend was an Irish girl. However, when we were punished, my punishment would be that much harder. She'd say that maybe I'd been naughtier, but I knew why it was.

I had my son when I was 20, and came to live with him in Brixton at my aunt's. She had her own house, and I had a room in it for me and Lorne. I only stayed two weeks in my first job. Babyminders in those days were often single mothers with three children to mind alongside their own. I took Lorne along, and the babyminder told me to put him on the couch. When I got back from work, there he was, still on the couch. This went on for four days. She couldn't take the children out because of all the stairs. I gave up my job and took him away – otherwise he would have turned into a robot. There were no nurseries then. He was nearly 3, and this was towards the end of the 1960s. So, with another woman from over the road, I started to take children myself. We used to take them to the park – what a nice sight! Sixteen little Black kids, marching through Brixton. Used to look good, one of us at the front, one behind!

Then I began as a voluntary youth worker. The council gave us a hut to get started, and as Lorne grew older, so my work changed, and I worked with older kids. I must have worked in every youth club in Brixton. All the kids there know me, and they are all young men and women now. All the schools and youth clubs there were run by white people, and there were hardly any Black teachers then. You'd never see or hear of them in the schools until Lorne was about 14. The kids would be amazed. They'd come home and say, 'Mummy, we've got a Black teacher!' or, 'There's a Black teacher at Stockwell Manor School.' It was so important to them.

I decided to start a youth project for Black youth run by Black people, but even now it's very hard to find Black youth projects with Black people in control. The one I work on now is managed by white people. We're often used as token workers in white-dominated clubs. There are now a few fully Black projects in London.

After seven years as a part-time voluntary worker, I went to college. I only went for the paper qualification because I couldn't get a full-time job without it. I found out that there have been Black workers in the field for up to twenty years, but they couldn't get decent jobs. The white man can't teach us anything; they're now trying to find out about Black youth work, yet we already know all about white youth work. They haven't even got their own act together, and yet they try to get ours together for us. The course was racist, but you can't expect any better. Racism is at its most effective when it's institutionalised in colleges, schools, hospitals, courts, prison and the police force.

Black women have been and still are doing their youth work at home and unacknowledged. Today Black parents are getting like white people in that they are only looking after their own. Many Black women are in the situation where they are 'Auntie' to from six to twenty young friends. They're called Auntie, not youth workers, and they are totally outside the system. It's only when Black women are confident about white youth workers that they'll let their girls go to the clubs. It's different for boys as they'd be more likely to let their boys out.

I work for an agency that I feel wants to be seen doing the work with Black youth because there's a lot of money around at the moment for so-called 'ethnic' work – money we never seem to see. But this agency doesn't really want to carry out Black projects with a total commitment to Black people because they are always trying to appease the immediate white community – and need to fund-raise from it. White people don't want to raise money for Black people unless they get something out of it, even if it is just to settle their guilty consciences. So while they'll soft-peddle with a 'multi-cultural' approach, they just won't commit themselves to a positive stand for Black youth. Many white people are frightened of young people, but doubly so if they are Black. The white staff I work with freak out if they see six or more Black young people.

As it is mainly boys who use the club, I make an effort to go out and get girls involved. I run a Black girls' group. We keep a Black perspective, and we're also anti-sexist, to improve the position of Black women. But on the whole my work isn't respected. It's popular with the youth, and the need is there, but the management won't recognise it. If they see you getting successful, involving a lot of Black young people, they get frightened. They don't want the popularity of my work to undermine the rest of the centre's work, which is mainly white. They accept that I'm a good worker, but I'm only accepted as a good Black worker, which to them is something less than a good white worker.

Racism is such a painful experience: in all my life I've never had even a short break from it. White people are not born racist, and they know in their hearts it is wrong. It is evil. You start to dig it out, like it was something rotten in the bark of a tree. And then you move on and dig out another bit. You move on and dig out a bit more . . . and by the time you are back to where you started, it's growing again. Like grass – always growing. This society is so comfortable about racism now. It's like an old jacket. It needs to take it off, and get used to being in a sweater – only they're not prepared to 'back off the jacket'. That's why Black people are angry. We make so much positive effort, but white people make no step at all. It's like a line that the white man wants me to walk up to, and when I reach it, he wants me to step over it for him. It doesn't matter how many steps you take, he's backing off, you still can't meet as an equal.

We say, 'The white people, them dread,' but in our hearts we know that opinions are forced on lots of whites from birth. I love the elderly people who come to the centre. They are all white. It doesn't matter to me so much that they're racist. Racism was instilled into them when they were young, when there wasn't anyone around to oppose it. It is possible to challenge them: if you respect people, and you see them do something wrong, you should tell them, as another human being. You shouldn't just assume people can't change because they are old. Old white people have learnt to live with change, have learnt to see Black people in different ways. But my organisation doesn't want to see that change, doesn't want to set time aside for those who work with the elderly to work out ways to counter racism. As a consequence, the old white people there see the centre as their territory, and won't open up to the Black elderly of the area. They send them up the road to the Black pensioners' group with the words, 'You wouldn't like it here.' That's always their opening and parting shot! When they come out with their racist remarks, I challenge them. I hope and trust in Jah for the strength and the inspiration for a good one-liner!

White people need to back off from those negative vibes. The expressions of racism are evil and violent, and Black people feel those vibes. Whites may think we don't know and feel them. But we have a saying: 'Them who feels it, knows it.'

CHAPTER 18

Making Gardens from Wildernesses

Norma Pitfield

I guess I was in love with my mother from childhood to her death. An only child, born when she was 35, I was forever fixed on her as the arbiter of my character, or rather my morality. A loving, indeed a dedicated mother, I believe now that she saw herself as the setter of standards and myself as the ever potential breaker of those. When, in 1954, I became an unmarried mother it was, in a sense, a triumph of her belief in my ability to disappoint her.

From that time onward the guilt I felt toward her fuelled a constant struggle to prove myself worthy in her eyes. The passionate love I also had for her, my awareness of her frustrated intellect and creativeness, kept her always in the forefront of my mind. Thus I spent a substantial proportion of my time with her, and when I wasn't with her I was worrying about her and struggling with anger and resentment.

Always dogged by bad health, her last decade was distressingly and increasingly painful. In spite of that she lived fully. There was a gallantry of spirit about her which attracted many people, and she was proud of her independence. She was buried on her eighty-first birthday. She had, with my father, come to live with me, very reluctantly, five months previously. I nursed her night and day over those last terrible months. She was the first person I had seen die, indeed the first person I had seen dead. Our intimacy over that time was complete. Although she resented her reliance upon me, she valued the fact that she could depend upon me. She fought desperately to live on, day by day, hour by hour, refusing to let go. Her way of dying stretched me to breaking point since it taxed my physical and emotional stamina to the ultimate. I fumed against her refusal to let go and release me from this final test. Yet I felt impelled to support her manner of death.

Scrupulously I performed every intimate personal service with passionate care, even though all my life I have found such tasks anathema. I would help her try to evacuate, devise ways to help her urinate, clear up vomit over and over again, then later rush to the bathroom to heave and heave.

Her death brought immense relief, but the guilt of feeling that relief added an intolerable dimension to my inconsolable grief. All this coincided with the onset of my menopause and of complex personal relationship problems. At that time I had also taken on a new and very responsible job. The job should have been a culmination of my working career giving, as it did, the opportunity to develop and put into practice my ideology about teaching my subject: art and design. Sadly my taking up the post coincided with all the changes and financial cuts in my particular field, teacher education.

I started the job in a very debilitated state, shocked, bereaved and physically at sixes and sevens. Everything was new, students, staff, the content of the course. I discovered there was some resentment at my appointment: the course had moved premises and nothing was ready. But the students were a delight, and despite everything the staff began generously to accept me. Later to my surprise I found that the students had little inkling of the strain of all the problems, and in retrospect I feel proud that, in spite of the constant panic I was experiencing inside my head, I was able to function professionally well enough.

While I was trying to cope at work my father was needing a lot of care at home. I was conscious of the strain his presence was inflicting on the people I lived with, even though I found a kind and efficient woman to care for him during the day. Looking back I see how amenable my father was until his sudden death eighteen months after my mother's. He had always been loving and supportive to me.

For some years I had spent holidays on the East Suffolk coast, an area I love. I had taken my parents there, my father just before his death. Remembering him saying how he wished I could have my own place there, I suddenly determined that I would buy a cottage from the proceeds of the sale of my parents' home. The search for somewhere suitable lifted me out of the depressive state the anxiety about my job and the problems at home were provoking. Having found the cottage I set to work on making it as peaceful and comfortable a haven as I could for my family, friends – but mainly for myself. I enjoy physical work. I also enjoy creating efficient and visually pleasing living space. In spite of menopausal problems I tackled the difficult, neglected garden and in quite a short space of time it looked well and, with the cottage, provided a comfortable and pleasing place to rest and work.

After this bout of energetic activity the depression returned in full force and threatened to overwhelm me. At the worst times I believed myself to be a fraud, likely at any time to be discovered as an inadequate sham at home and at work. I had been given a commission to write a book. The cottage seemed to provide the ideal quiet retreat for this purpose on my weekend visits. As the date for completion, the end of the summer vacation, drew near, I settled in and tried to get down to finish the work. But the depression was at its worst and my thoughts suicidal.

I felt that the book's potential failure would at last reveal the truth, my fraudulence, poverty of ideas, incompetence, unworthiness! One dreadful morning I rushed into the garden in the pouring rain, frenetically hacking down bushes and thorns on a steep and slippery bank in an effort to prevent myself from some terrible deed of self-destruction. I paced the garden for hours, day after day, trying in a way that was *physically* painful to focus my mind and evolve some plan of self-salvation. Grimly I imposed a regime of writing, gardening, writing, playing my piano, writing, drawing in the evenings, and then writing into the early hours. Sticking to the plan in an utterly joyless way the deadline was met and I flew to New York to meet some friends as pre-arranged. I remember spending the flight trying to suppress my conviction that, while in America, all those miles away from home, I would fall seriously ill, or go mad.

Neither happened. Instead I returned to work, edited and re-edited the book, and tried to cope with ever-increasing difficulties at work. Cuts in staff and facilities were made. I was involved in endless complex meetings and the preparation of detailed documentation arguing for my course and submitted time and time again to various supervising committees. All this involved constant rewriting late at night on top of a heavy teaching and administrative schedule. Each committee meeting was a nightmare. I was having to articulate in detail reasons for the way the course was taught and run, indeed for its very existence, a huge responsibility towards many people. While my immediate colleagues and I felt confidence in what we were doing, I had always known that my immediate superiors would have preferred a more traditional approach. Now I discerned open hostility and, as I saw it, of lack of professional support for the innovatory nature of our work. At one meeting I was publicly insulted by one man's rudeness; based on his own well-known prejudices and ignorance about art education. No one challenged him, though afterwards in private there were commiserations. To me this signalled that my work world was collapsing and I went home convinced that I could take no more.

From that time, as I wept and fumed I believe I began to recover from the years of depression. For as long as I could remember my work had been where I felt I functioned well. Divorced as it was from my mother's sphere of influence, I had enjoyed my competence free from guilt and doubt. With my mother's death and the onset of the menopause, due to either, both, who knows, the eroding canker of uncertainty started to eat into that aspect of my life. It also coincided with the unhappy state of affairs in higher education. I have seen many professional colleagues go under, giving up work, becoming seriously ill, suffering mental breakdowns, even prematurely dying. My own health often faltered under the pressure, with the return of the persistent asthma I'd suffered in my 20s.

As it turned out I was extremely fortunate. Premature retirement or voluntary redundancy was on offer on good terms. Originally I'd refused to entertain the idea. I'd always been convinced that I would want to teach forever. Moreover to get a pension at my early age seemed immoral. Now I thought again. Life without a job or work imposed from outside seemed, to my surprise, a definite possibility. Having my cottage had proved to me I could function alone, at least for a considerable proportion of the time. It had also confirmed my love of living in the country.

All the possibilities were discussed at length with my partner, who generously backed me fully in my decision to leave work. Within a year we sold our beloved home and acquired a very much more modest London base, sold the cottage and bought for me a house in a small country town large enough for me to run the occasional residential art course.

I have lived in that house for five months now and experience once again a pleasure in my ability to create a place where people love to come to stay. Another garden is in the process of being created. I am learning new art skills and practising old ones. For years any political involvement had been fraught with problems of time and energy. At 52 I find I am able to join campaigns again and work for them in a consistent and reliable way. When I was younger I was very active in the peace movement. Now I've joined again, and I'm helping in CLAM (Coastal League Against Missiles), which is affiliated to CND. I've been to

Greenham Common and I support and admire the stand being made there. And I've rejoined the Labour Party.

I am genuinely enjoying meeting new people, establishing new friendships and actively enjoying old ones. For the first time since before the menopause I feel confident to sustain and cherish friends. This is not to say that for all those years I have been friendless – far from it. My contacts through the women's movement have given me loving support through so many traumas. The difference is that for a long time I construed such support as compassion and pity. Now I have the time and confidence to think about friends dispassionately *and* passionately, free from any turmoil of guilt or doubt. I feel justified in planning and using my time according to my own decisions and energies.

I have truly started again, a new kind of life.

Eight years ago when my mother died, to my surprise and disappointment there was no sense of the liberation I'd expected. On the contrary I too believed I had begun to die. Everything for a time conspired to reinforce this conviction, ill health, evidence of physical ageing, the running down of sexual responses in myself and from others. Older women are very conditioned to feeling self-disgust and the physical symptoms of the menopause can be construed to reinforce this. I suffered not only heavy bleeding, severe headaches, hot flushes, uncertainty of mood but also water retention which caused swelling of hands, feet, abdomen and face. My otherwise kindly doctor could only offer HRT (hormone replacement therapy) of which I was afraid. All the reading I did on the menopause, especially by women, advocated keeping fit, slim, active.

Unable to manage any of this I felt, like many others I'm sure, even more of a failure. Later I developed severe neuralgia and arthritis, very frightening, and extremely painful. But these illnesses took me to an acupuncturist. I gained relief and, through his confidence in me, the strength to try self-help in the form of careful diet, exercise and visualisation. I also sought psychotherapy which provided the opportunity to think and talk about my mental and emotional bad, and good, habits. Gradually mourning for my youthful body gave way to pride in my older one. When I joined the Older Feminist Network, the beauty and strength of older women became more and more apparent and admirable.

Even though those eight years since my mother's death have been so difficult, I now see them as very productive. They saw some of my best and most informed teaching. A book was written. I made and exhibited drawings. I made a garden out of a wilderness. I acquired many friendships which I know to be lasting. Not only that: stretching ahead is the exciting prospect of a new way of being.

Many things have been left out of this account, most significantly the complexities and richness of my closest personal relationships. But this story is about an equally important aspect of life – the experience of oneself. We all live partially in reaction to the needs, experiences and demands of others, many of us completely so, especially women. Getting to know and appreciate oneself I now see as an important priority and an exciting and stimulating adventure and I count myself lucky to have the opportunity to embark on a new life as an older woman in a positive frame of mind.

The menopause and the depressive state that often seems to accompany it for so many women could be seen as a change of life in the best sense. It so often marks changes other than the physical. The death of parents, the departure of children, could be the end of an era of succouring and serving on a day-to-day basis. My work too had this nurturing dimension. Now I know I did my best for those others. I can rue my failures and rejoice in my successes, but I no longer dwell upon them.

References

These notes are to supplement the text, and are not meant as a guide to organisations, or a listing. All the books, groups and organisations mentioned below, listed alphabetically, are referred to by contributors in their pieces. If they are already fully explained in the main part of the book, they do not appear below.

A Woman's Place (formerly the London Women's Liberation Workshop). The central London women's liberation centre. Drop in for information, books, pamphlets, etc. Also a meeting place for women's groups. Will inform you of your local groups (London and nationally, also some international information). Visit, write (sae) or phone 01-836 6081. Women only. Hungerford House, Victoria Embankment, London WC2. (See page 81).

Campaign for Nuclear Disarmament (also referred to in the book and generally as CND) Long-established campaign, with many local groups. The London office will inform you: 11 Goodwin Street, London N4 (01-263 0977). (See pages 21, 43, 74, 78, 154, 169).

City Literary Institute Centre for adult education of various kinds, range of interesting evening and part-time courses. Details from: The Secretary, City Literary Institute, Stukeley Street, London WC2. (See page 93).

Consciousness-raising groups, also generally known as CR groups. These are usually small groups of women who meet on a regular basis in their locality to discuss matters related to their lives as women (e.g. health, work, relationships, family, sexuality, etc). The intention is to encourage each other, by exchanging experiences and ideas, to build a greater understanding of the conditions influencing women's lives and a greater confidence to counter sexism and/or related oppressions. Sometimes these groups develop into campaigning groups. There are also 'special' groups for particular groups of women: Black women, lesbians, working-class women, women with disabilities, younger women, older women, etc. looking at their specific issues in a consciousness-raising setting. You can find out if there is a general or special CR group in your locality by sending an sae to A Woman's Place (see above). You can also advertise (free in some cases) to find or start one in the classified advertisement section of *Spare Rib* magazine (see below). There are hundreds of groups all over the country, with new ones starting up all the time. (See pages 57, 59, 60, 68, 75, 76, 81, 87, 122, 123, 124).

Co-operative Women's Guild This was founded in 1883, as part of the national and international Co-operative movement. It carried out pioneering work for women, with involvement in the suffrage movement, peace movement, hunger marches, and all major equal rights struggles. It was the first organisation to pass a resolution on abortion (1934). A book documenting its history and achievements, *Caring and Sharing* by Jean Gaffin, was published in 1983 to celebrate its centenary. Still going strong: you can find out about your nearest group by sending a sae to The Co-operative Women's Guild, 342 Hoe Street, London E17. (See page 16).

Friends of the Earth This campaigns for greater protection of the natural environment, and will inform you of local groups/similar organisations: 377 City Road, London EC1 (01-837 0731). (See pages 21, 154).

Greenham Women The over-all name for the women's peace and anti-nuclear action which centres on Greenham Common Air Base (near Newbury in Berkshire) where the first cruise missiles were sited. There are many groups nationally, taking action locally, nationally, and at Greenham. For details of local groups, send sae to London Greenham Office, 144 Caledonian Road, London N1 (01-833 2831/2). The Peace Camp: USAF Greenham Common, Newbury, Berkshire. (See pages 21, 76, 124, 170).

Hillcroft College For women wishing to study, and perhaps prepare for college/university entrance, who do not necessarily have O- and A-level passes. Residential, but you can live out too. Grants (at time this book was published . . . cutbacks may ensue, so check). For details of full- and part-time courses, send sae to General Office, Hillcroft College, Southbank, Surbiton, Surrey. (See pages 58, 59, 60).

Jewish Feminist Groups Send sae c/o Sisterwrite Bookshop, 190 Upper St., London N1. Also for details of Jewish Feminist Newsletter. (See pages 76, 77).

Humanist Groups and societies meet in many areas nationally. Details from The British Humanist Association, 13 Prince of Wales Terrace, London W8 (01-937 2341). (See pages 68, 69).

Mary Daly is an American radical feminist theorist, and the book Marjorie refers to in her piece is *Gyn/Ecology*. (See page 85).

National Abortion Campaign Long-standing feminist organisation, fighting for a woman's right to choose (whether or not to have children) and giving many women help and advice. Also organised many campaigns against government attempts to make it more difficult for women to get abortions. At crisis times, hundreds of groups organised nationally. In 1983, split into two groups, one continuing to focus only on abortion rights, the other on the whole range of connected issues (fertility, contraception, sexuality, etc.). Single-issue organisation: National Abortion Campaign (NAC), 75 Kingsway, London WC2 (01-405 4801). Broad-based campaign: Women's Reproductive Rights Information Centre (WRRIC), 52-54 Featherstone Street, London N1 (01-251 6332/3). (See page 56).

Older Feminist Network Has been going and growing, nationally, since 1981. Women from both London and other areas meet regularly about ten times a year in London on Saturdays. There is no formal membership, and new women are always welcome at these meetings. Dates and venue are advertised in *Spare Rib* (see below) and in the Older Feminist Newsletter, which is brought out regularly by the Network, on subscription. There are also several small groups (mainly consciousness-raising, see above) meeting in London and nationally. Details from Older Feminist Network, c/o A Woman's Place, as above. You can also advertise (free) in *Spare Rib* to find/start a local group. (See pages 60, 87, 146, 171).

Outwrite Monthly feminist newspaper with an anti-racist, anti-imperialist perspective. Details from *Outwrite* at Oxford House, Derbyshire Street, London E2 (01-729 4575). (See page 76).

Rape Crisis Centres have been set up by women in many areas of Britain, and in Ireland. Many have 24-hour answering services on which you can leave a message at any time. Help and support for women who have been raped or sexually assaulted (including those attacked in the past). Ring one of these numbers (or write) to find the nearest centre to you: *London RCC* 01-837 1600 (24-hour line); 01-278 3956 (office hours); PO Box 69, London WC1X 9NJ. *Aberdeen RCC* 0224 575560, Monday 6-8 p.m. Thursday 7-9 p.m. PO Box 123, Aberdeen.

South Wales RCC 0222 373181, Monday and Thursday 7-10 p.m., Wednesday 11-2 p.m. Box 17, 108 Salisbury Road, Cardiff. *Belfast RCC* 0232 249696, Monday to Friday 1-6 p.m. Tuesday to Friday 7.30-10 p.m. PO Box 46, Belfast BT2 7AR. Dublin RCC Dublin 601 470, 7 day a week 24-hour service. 2 Lower Pembroke Street, Dublin 2. (See page 57).

Sappho Was a Right-On Woman by Sidney Abbott and Barbara Love. American book. A look at the way lesbians are changing in society, both before and after feminist and gay-rights consciousness. (See page 146).

Rosie the Riveter A documentary film. Four women (in the USA) talking about their experiences during and after the Second World War as workers in shipyards, ammunition factories and foundries. Colour. Lasts one hour. To hire: 16mm version, £35 plus VAT, VHS £20 plus VAT, from The Other Cinema, 79 Wardour Street, London W1 (01-734 8508). (See page 47).

Shelter is a national campaign for the homeless, with its main office at 157 Waterloo Road, London SE1 (01-633 9377). (See page 146).

Spare Rib is a monthly women's liberation magazine (news, features, letters, reviews, what's on) available from newsagents or on subscription. If not in your newsagent, tell them the distributor is Comag. Details of subscriptions, etc. from Spare Rib, 27 Clerkenwell Close, London EC1 0AT (01-253 9792). (See page 76).

The Female Eunuch by Germaine Greer, is a feminist book setting out some of the basic issues of women becoming liberated from men's domination. Concentrates mainly on roles and stereotypes. Two other similarly influential books of the same year (1971): Shulamith Firestone's *Dialectic of Sex* (strong critiques of the family, motherhood, psychology, and the relationship between the sexes) and Kate Millet's *Sexual Politics*, an important basic book setting out the terms, as she saw them, of sexual politics and liberation. All well-known and well-read basic women's liberation texts, perhaps the most widely read three in the early 1970s. (See page 75).

Women Against Racism and Fascism (often known as WARF) was active in the late 1970s and early 80s, but no longer exists in this form. As the name implies, it was formed to consciousness-raise, educate and take action to counter racism, imperialism and fascism, and there were groups in most areas nationally. (See page 75).

Women's Aid Another feminist initiative of the 1970s, still going strong: set up refuges for battered women throughout Britain, and pioneered work on domestic violence from men towards women and children. Women's Aid Federation (England), 52-54 Featherstone Street, London N1 (01-251 6429). Also WAFE at c/o Manchester Women's Centre, 116 Portland Street, Manchester (061-228 1069). Northern Ireland Women's Aid Federation: 143 University Street, Belfast BT7 1HP (0232 249041/249358). Scottish Women's Aid: 11 St Colme Street, Edinburgh EH3 6AA (031-225 3321). Welsh Women's Aid: Incentive House, Adam Street, Cardiff (0222 462291). Dublin Family Aid: c/o PO Box 791, Dublin 6 (Dublin 961002). You can find out where your nearest refuge is by contacting the nearest main office. (See page 81).

Further references. Not comprehensive, but a few suggestions, based on matters raised in the book.

Books by/for/about older women There are quite a few! They are usually in stock at feminist/radical bookshops, or you can order them, or ask for them at your library. Two London-based feminist bookshops run mail-order services: Sisterwrite Bookshop, 190 Upper Street, London N1 (01-226 9782); Silver Moon, 68 Charing Cross Road, London WC2

(01-836 7906). If you send Sisterwrite or Silver Moon an sae asking for a list of older women's books, they'll send you a list of what they currently have in stock, fiction and non-fiction.

Women's Studies If you're interested in women's studies courses (at any level) write for details nationally to: Feminist Library, First Floor, Hungerford House, Victoria Embankment, London WC2 for their book of courses; also contact Workers' Educational Association Women's Studies Newsletter, 9 Upper Berkeley Street, London W1 (01-402 5608 or 061-325 9972) to find out what relevant WEA courses are in your area – or how to set one up.

Other useful handbooks and information

Women Rule OK, National Extension College. Contacts for women on education, work, health, living independently, with a guide to further reading.

Menopause: A Positive Approach, Rosetta Reitz (1979).

Female Cycles, Paula Weideger (1978), also contains material on menopause.

A Housing Rights Handbook, Marion Cutting (1979). Includes information on housing problems, on breakdown of marriage.

Back to Work: A Practical Guide for Women, Cathy Moulder and Pat Sheldon (1979). Careers opportunities for qualified and unqualified women, and gives further addresses.

Breaking Up: A Practical Guide to Separation and Divorce, Rosemary Brown (1980).

How To Conduct Your Own Divorce, Gil Friedman (1975).

Women's Rights: A Practical Guide, Anna Coote and Tess Gill (1974, but revised and updated several times). Excellent basic handbook, includes tax, social security, divorce, immigration, employment, etc.

Handbook for Widows, June Hemer and Ann Stanyer. What to do, and organisations.

All the above available from Sisterwrite Bookshop, Send sae for current prices.

Lesbians There is a married lesbians' group meeting regularly in London, and see below for older lesbians. For any information concerning lesbians (including help and advice) phone Lesbian Line. Branches all over the country: phone the nearest one to you below for details: London 01-251 6911, or write BM Box 1514, London WC1N 3XX; Sheffield 0742 581238, or write PO Box 162 IUD, Sheffield 1; Glasgow 041-248 4596, or write GLL, PO Box 57, Glasgow; Cardiff 0222 374051; Derry (Cara Friend) 0504 263120. If any of these lines are closed, it is possible to ring London Gay Switchboard 01-837 7324, open 24 hours a day, seven days a week, for gay women and men.

Older Lesbians Support Network (and newsletter). Founded spring 1984. London and national, meeting monthly in London, plus smaller support groups/networks as necessary. Details, send sae to London Friend, 274 Upper Street, London N1.

Black women's groups Contact the Black Women's Centre, 41a Stockwell Green, London SW9 (enclose sae), tel. 01-274 9220 for details of local groups. A Woman's Place (see above) also has a list (sae) of groups/centres.

Women with disabilities Sisters Against Disablement, London-based feminist network: contact rotates, so ask A Woman's Place (above); Liberation Network of People with Disabilities, c/o Townsend House, Green Lanes, Marshfield, Chippenham, Wilts.; Gemma (lesbians with and without disabilities), newsletter, penfriends, support. You can send your enquiries in print, braille or cassette. BM Box 5700, London WC1N 3XX.

For a very full list of groups organised around women's matters, see the annually published *Spare Rib* Diary, or other radical diaries with a women's perspective.

For low-price pamphlets on pensioners' rights and issues, contact your local Age Concern, a national organisation, whose address will be in your telephone book. They will also advise you on pensioners' rights groups in your locality. Or send sae to Age Concern, Bernard Sunley House, Pitcairn Road, Mitcham, Surrey (01-640 5431).